CURITY MAP

evere Food Insecurity

2.1.2

ce: FAO, IFAD, UNICEF, WFP and WHO. 2022. *The State of Food Security and Nutrition in the World 2022. Repurposing food and agricultural es to make healthy diets more affordable*. Data are available on FAOSTAT (**https://www.fao.org/faostat/en/#data/FS**)

出典　国際連合食糧農業機関（FAO）

Open Seas

for Global Friendships III

監修 　上智大学名誉教授　吉田　研作
　　　上智大学教授　　　藤田　保

BUN-EIDO

CONTENTS

■ **FAO FOOD INSECURITY MAP** ［前見返し］

■ 📷 **What do you see?** ［後見返し］

LESSON STEPS

CAN-DO
listen / read / talk / exchange opinions / write
LESSON のテーマにそって, **聞く / 読む / 話す / 意見を交わす / 書く** 練習の目標です.

Part 1

Let's Listen 1 🎧 **D** テーマに関連したモデル会話を聞いて質問に答え, 内容を理解します.

ANSWER THE QUESTIONS 会話のあとで〈質問文〉が英語で読まれます.

Let's Read 1 📖 **D** 前ページの Let's Listen 1 を文字で確認し, 内容を理解します.

Words & Phrases Let's Read を理解するための語句や表現

KEY PHRASES Let's Read の注目表現

Let's Practice 1 2 👥 **D** Let's Read 1 や KEY PHRASES などをペアやグループで練習をします.

Let's Talk 1 💬 **R** モデル会話を使い, 相手に質問したり, お互いに意見を交わす練習をします.

Toolbox Let's Talk で話すための語句や表現

Let's Listen 2 🎧 **D** Let's Listen 1 より長めの会話を聞いて, 質問に答え, 内容を理解します.

ANSWER THE QUESTIONS 会話のあとで〈質問文〉が英語で読まれます.

Let's Read 2 📖 **D** 前ページの Let's Listen 2 に関連し, いろいろなグラフを用いた英文 (4課を除く) を読み, 質問に答えます.

Let's Write ✏️ **R** テーマに関して, 自分の意見などを書く練習をします.

Let's Talk 2 💬 **R** Let's Write で書いた内容について, ペアやグループで意見を交わし, まとめて発表します.

📷 **What do you see?** 写真に写っている人物や内容について, 説明をしたり, 話し合う活動をします.

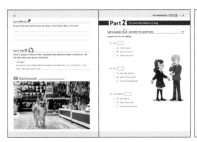
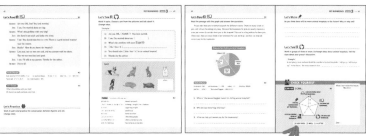

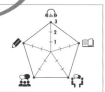

🏔 **CHECK YOURSELF**

LESSON の終わりに, 5項目の自己評価 (3段階)
"CAN-DO チェック" を行いましょう.

■ Part 2

Let's Listen 🎧   **D** Part1 Let's Listen1 よりやや情報量の多いモデル会話を聞いて内容を理解します.

   ANSWER THE QUESTIONS   会話のあとで〈質問文〉が英語で読まれます.

Let's Read 1 📖   **D** 前ページの Let's Listen を文字で確認し, 内容を理解します.

  Words & Phrases   Let's Read を理解するための語句や表現

  KEY PHRASES   Let's Read の注目表現

Let's Practice 👥   **D** Let's Read1 や KEY PHRASES などをペアやグループで練習をします.

Let's Talk 1 💬   **R** モデル会話を使い, 相手に質問したり, お互いに意見を交わす練習をします.

  Toolbox   Let's Talk で話すための語句や表現

Let's Read 2 📖   **D** 少し長めの英文を読み, 質問に答えます. 1, 2, 3, 5, 6, 8課はグラフを用いた英文です.

Let's Write ✏   **R** テーマに関して, 自分の意見などを書く練習をします.

Let's Talk 2 💬   **R** Let's Write で書いた内容について, ペアやグループで意見を交わし, まとめて発表します.

🔊 … Let's Listen, Let's Read, Words & Phrases, KEY PHRASES, Toolbox には音声があります.

D … Display 度の高い活動：質問に対する答えを知った上で, あえてまた質問し, それに答えるような活動.

R … Referential 度の高い活動：新たな情報を知るために質問し, それに答えるような活動.

MAIN CHARACTERS

Friends & Teachers

Koyama Yumi

Eric Chen

Asakura Sayaka

Kimura Shizuka

Honda Nanami

Oliver King

Noguchi Ayame

Honda Kentaro

Uchikawa Kana

Jon Taylor

Sakamoto Hayato

Hara Rikuya

8

SMARTPHONE/TABLET

● アクセス方法

A-1 右のQRコードを読み取るOpen Seas Ⅲ のトップページにアクセスできます．

A-2 トップページ，または画面右上のメニュー をタップし，はじめたいLessonを選択します．

B 各Lessonとも，一番はじめのCAN-DOページ写真 右下にあるQRコードを読み取ると，そのLessonに アクセスできます．

 A-1
 A-2
 B

1 CAN-DO

各Lessonの目標を確認しましょう．

7 CHECK YOURSELF

3段階で自己評価を行い，その 結果を先生やクラスメイトと共有 しましょう．

2 Let's Listen

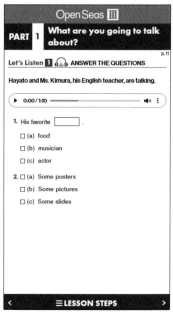

モデル会話を聞いて質問に答え ましょう．

3 Let's Read

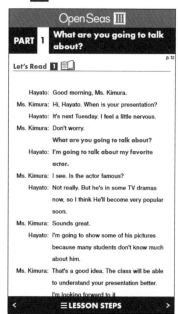

Let's Listenを文字で確認（Let's Read①）したり，Lessonのテーマ を扱った英文（Let's Read②）を 読んだりしてみましょう．

How to Use Open Seas with Your Smartphone/Tablet

4 Let's Practice

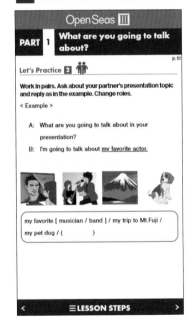

ポイントとなる表現の練習を
しましょう.

5 Let's Talk

自分自身のことについて, ペア
やグループでやりとりする練習
をしましょう. Toolbox の語句
を参考にして練習しましょう.

6 Let's Write

COPY をタップし, 入力した
内容を email, SMS などで送信し
ましょう.

MAKING A PRESENTATION

CAN-DO

In this lesson, you will...

 listen **to talks about topics in everyday life.**

 read **about topics in everyday life.**

 talk **about topics in everyday life.**

 exchange **opinions about a good presentation.**

 write **your opinions about a good presentation.**

Part 1   What are you going to talk about?

Let's Listen 1 ANSWER THE QUESTIONS

Hayato and Ms. Kimura, his English teacher, are talking.

1. His favorite ▭

    ☐ (a) food

    ☐ (b) musician

    ☐ (c) actor

2. ☐ (a) Some posters

    ☐ (b) Some pictures

    ☐ (c) Some slides

Let's Read 1 📖 🔊

Hayato: Good morning, Ms. Kimura.

Ms. Kimura: Hi, Hayato. When is your presentation?

Hayato: It's next Tuesday. I feel a little nervous.

Ms. Kimura: Don't worry. What are you going to talk about?

Hayato: I'm going to talk about my favorite actor.

Ms. Kimura: I see. Is the actor famous?

Hayato: Not really. But he's in some TV dramas now, so I think he'll become very popular soon.

Ms. Kimura: Sounds great.

Hayato: I'm going to show some pictures of him because many students don't know much about him.

Ms. Kimura: That's a good idea. The class will be able to understand your presentation better. I'm looking forward to it.

Hayato: Thank you, Ms. Kimura.

Words & Phrases 🔊

feel nervous 緊張している　　Don't worry. 心配ないですよ。　　Not really. それほどでもない。

TV dramas テレビドラマ

KEY PHRASES 🔊

What are you going to talk about?

I'm going to talk about my favorite actor.

Let's Practice 1 👥

Work in pairs and practice the conversation between Hayato and Ms. Kimura. Change roles.

Let's Practice 2

Work in pairs. Ask about your partner's presentation topic and reply as in the example. Change roles.

〈 Example 〉

> A: What are you going to talk about in your presentation?
>
> B: I'm going to talk about <u>my favorite actor</u>.

> my favorite [musician/band] / my trip to Mt. Fuji / my pet dog / (   )

Let's Talk 1

Work in pairs and talk about your presentation.

〈 Example 〉

> A: What are you going to talk about in your presentation?
>
> B: I'm going to talk about _____.
>
> A: Are you going to use anything in your talk?
>
> B: I'm going to use _____.
>
> A: I'm looking forward to your presentation.
>
> B: Thank you.

Toolbox 🔊

〈 話す内容の例 〉　　好きな食べ物 my favorite food

　　　　　　　　　　（私の町の）好きなお祭り my favorite festival（in my town）

　　　　　　　　　　私の家族 my family　　　私の宝物 my treasure

〈 発表で使うものの例 〉写真／絵はがき／スライド／グラフ some [photos / picture postcards / slides / graphs]

　　　　　　　　　　コンピュータ a computer　　　大きなスクリーン a large screen

Let's Listen 2 ANSWER THE QUESTIONS

Jon and Ayame are talking.

1. ☐ (a) Her favorite singer

   ☐ (b) Healthy food

   ☐ (c) Popular pets

2. ☐ (a) His favorite movie

   ☐ (b) Healthy food

   ☐ (c) Popular pets

3. ☐ (a) Getting information on the internet takes time.

   ☐ (b) Information on the internet is not always true.

   ☐ (c) Using the internet is sometimes expensive.

Let's Read 2

Read the passage with the graph and answer the questions.

In the English class next month, the students are going to make presentations. Today, the teacher showed seven topics and asked the students to choose one of them. The students are happy with the topics because all the topics are familiar. They think that there will be a lot of things to talk about. In next week's class, they are going to write their drafts for the presentations.

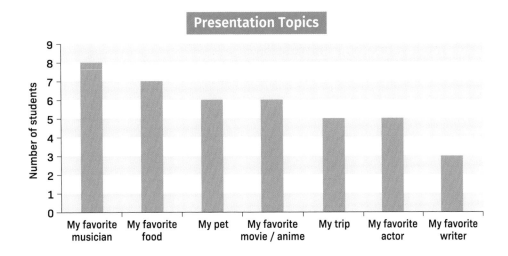

Presentation Topics

topic 話題,トピック　　familiar なじみのある　　drafts 原稿

1. Which is the most popular topic of presentation?

_____.

2. Why are the students happy with the topics?

_____.

3. What will the students do in next week's class?

_____.

Let's Write ✏️

Choose one of the topics in the graph on page 15 for your presentation.

I'm going to talk about _____

because _____ .

Let's Talk 2 💬👥

Work in groups of three or more. Ask each other about the presentation topic.
Tell the class about your group's discussion.

〈Example〉

In our group, two students have chosen "My favorite food," one student has chosen "My favorite musician," and one student has chosen "My pet."

📷 What do you see? Look at this photo and talk about it.

Part 2 Please look at this picture.

Let's Listen 🎧 ANSWER THE QUESTIONS 🔊

Listen to Rikuya's presentation.

1. ☐ (a) The food he wants to eat

   ☐ (b) The country he wants to visit

   ☐ (c) The pet he wants to have

2. ☐ (a) Two

   ☐ (b) Three

   ☐ (c) Four

3. Because he wants to ☐ in a foreign country

   ☐ (a) work

   ☐ (b) have friends

   ☐ (c) learn many things

Let's Read **1** 📖 🔊

Read Rikuya's presentation.

> Hello, everyone.
>
> Today, I'm going to talk about the country that I want to visit in the future. Please look at this picture. What country is this? Yes, it's Australia. There are many reasons why I want to go there. Let me tell you about two of them.
>
> First, Australia has a lot of beautiful beaches and nature. I want to enjoy outdoor activities there. Second, I want to learn about the culture. I think people there have different lifestyles and different ways of thinking. In order to learn many things in Australia, I want to study English hard.
>
> Thank you very much for listening.

Words & Phrases 🔊

outdoor activities 野外活動（activity-activities）　　lifestyles ライフスタイル, 生活様式
ways of thinking 考え方　　in order to... …するために

KEY PHRASES 🔊

I want to visit Australia in the future.
There are many reasons why...
Let me tell you about two of them.
First,...
Second,...

Let's Practice

Work in groups of three or more and take turns reading Rikuya's presentation aloud. Try to have natural eye contact with other students.

Let's Talk 1

Work in pairs and talk about the country that you want to visit in the future.
Change roles.

〈 Example 〉

A: I want to visit _____ in the future.

Why? First, _____.

Second, _____.

How about you?

B: I want to visit _____ in the future.

First, _____.

Second, _____.

Toolbox 🔊

…を見たい	I want to see...
…を食べたい	I want to eat...
…をしたい	I want to do...
…を学びたい	I want to learn...
…の写真をとりたい	I want to take pictures of...

自然（nature）	beautiful [beaches / rivers / mountains]
観光地（tourist spot）	a famous [building / tower / museum / monuments]
食べ物（food）	[local / traditional] food
活動（activity）	sports / camping / fishing / shopping

Britain

China

Egypt

Korea

Switzerland

The United States

Let's Read 2 📖

🔊

Read the passage with the graph and answer the questions.

Before we make a presentation, we need to practice many times. If we practice a lot, we will not make many mistakes and will not feel too nervous.

There are some important points to remember in making a good presentation. Mr. King, the English teacher, asked his students about the points. The graph shows the students' answers. The ability to make a good presentation will be important in the future, so we need to learn how to make a good presentation.

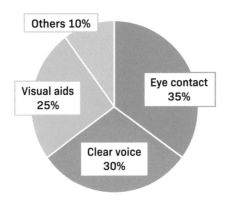

Important Points in Making a Good Presentation

Others 10%

Visual aids 25%

Eye contact 35%

Clear voice 30%

Words & Phrases

🔊

the ability to... …する能力   eye contact 視線を合わせること   clear voice はっきりした声
visual aids 視覚資料（イラスト, 写真, スライドなど）

1. The students think that _____ is the most important thing when making a presentation.

2. Why do we need to practice a lot before making a presentation?

_____.

3. Why do we need to learn how to make a good presentation?

_____.

Let's Write ✏️

What is the most important thing for you to do to make a good presentation? Why?

_____

_____

_____

Let's Talk 2

Work in groups of three or more. Exchange ideas about making a good presentation.
Tell the class about your group's discussion.

〈 Example 〉

In our group, two students think eye contact is the most important point in making a good
presentation. One student thinks a clear voice is the most important.

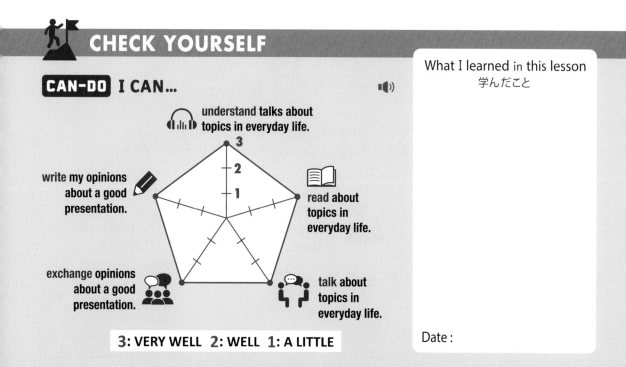

CHECK YOURSELF

CAN-DO I CAN... 🔊

understand talks about
topics in everyday life.

write my opinions
about a good
presentation.

read about
topics in
everyday life.

exchange opinions
about a good
presentation.

talk about
topics in
everyday life.

3: VERY WELL 2: WELL 1: A LITTLE

What I learned in this lesson
学んだこと

Date :

Lesson 2
TRADITIONAL CULTURES

CAN-DO

In this lesson, you will...

 listen to talks about traditional cultures.

> read about traditional cultures.

> talk about traditional cultures.

> exchange opinions about traditional cultures.

> write your opinions about traditional cultures.

Part 1 | Have you listened to traditional Japanese music?

Let's Listen 1 🎧 ANSWER THE QUESTIONS 🔊

Sayaka and Mr. King are talking.

1. He is [   ] .

☐ (a) listening to music

☐ (b) playing the *sanshin*

☐ (c) singing with Sayaka

2. Because [   ]

☐ (a) it is a traditional Japanese instrument

☐ (b) she plays it every day

☐ (c) it has a beautiful tone

Let's Read 1 📖 🔊

Sayaka: Hi, Mr. King. What are you listening to?

Mr. King: Music from Okinawa. The sound of the *sanshin* and rhythm are really nice. Would you like to hear it?

Sayaka: Yes, thanks. (Sayaka listens to the music.)

Nice music. It makes me remember the blue ocean in summer.

Mr. King: Really? That's interesting. We don't have anything like *sanshin* in New Zealand.

It's interesting to listen to music from different countries.

Sayaka: Have you listened to other traditional Japanese instruments?

Mr. King: Not yet. What do you recommend?

Sayaka: I like the sound of the koto, a Japanese harp. It can make soft flowing sounds as well as short strong sounds. I like the beautiful tone. Why don't you listen to it on the internet? I'm sure you can find songs on an online music channel.

Mr. King: That sounds great. I'll check it tonight.

Words & Phrases 🔊

rhythm リズム   remember... …を思い起こす   recommend 勧める   tone 音色

KEY PHRASES 🔊

It's interesting to listen to music from different countries.

Why don't you listen to it on the internet?

Let's Practice 1 👥

Work in pairs and practice the conversation between Sayaka and Mr. King.
Change roles.

Let's Practice 2

Work in pairs. Ask about your partner's experience and reply as in the example. Change roles.

〈Example〉

A: Have you listened to traditional Japanese music?

B: [Yes. I have listened to shamisen before. / No, I haven't. I want to listen to it.]

play the koto

carry a *mikoshi*

write a haiku

wear a kimono

Let's Talk 1

Work in pairs and talk about traditional Japanese experiences. Change roles.

〈Example〉

A: Have you been to a summer festival?

B: Yes.

A: Did you enjoy it?

B: Yes. There were so many delicious foods.

A: I'm glad you had a great time.

A: Have you been to a summer festival?

B: No.

A: Why don't you go to one? It's fun.

B: Maybe I will.

A: I think you'll enjoy it.

Toolbox

神社にお参りする visit a shrine

習字/書道をする do calligraphy

お好み焼きを作る make *okonomiyaki*

生け花に挑戦する try ikebana

和太鼓を演奏する play Japanese drums

どれかに行ってみる go to one

試してみる/食べてみる try it

Let's Listen 2 🎧 ANSWER THE QUESTIONS 🔊

Nanami and Rikuya are talking.

1. He wants to [   ] in high school.

   ☐ (a) apply for a short study abroad program

   ☐ (b) study the Ainu native culture

   ☐ (c) learn about the Ryukyu Kingdom

2. ☐ (a) Canada or New Zealand

   ☐ (b) Hokkaido

   ☐ (c) Okinawa

3. ☐ (a) Canada and New Zealand

   ☐ (b) Hokkaido

   ☐ (c) Okinawa

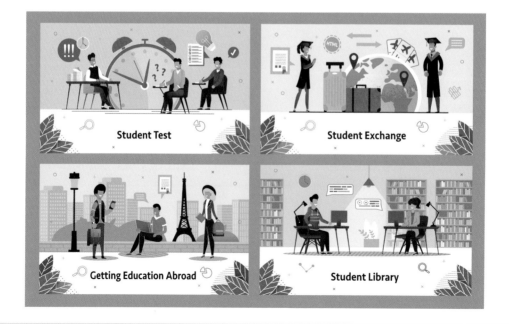

Student Test

Student Exchange

Getting Education Abroad

Student Library

Let's Read **2** 📖

Read the passage with the graph and answer the questions.

Hayato went to a tourist desk in Asakusa with his friend from Australia. They asked a tour guide, "What activities are popular among foreign tourists?" Here are the results of what they were told.

The most popular activity was "rent a kimono." Many visitors enjoy the beautiful designs and enjoy posing for photos dressed in kimono. It is also popular because each person can choose their own obi to match their kimono.

The second most popular activity was "watch a sumo match." Sumo is the national sport of Japan. Many visitors are amazed by the big and powerful sumo wrestlers.

Last of all, about the same number of people chose these three activities: attending a tea ceremony, staying at a temple, and going to a hot spring. They are all activities unique to Japan. It would be interesting for foreign tourists to experience these things during their visit to Japan.

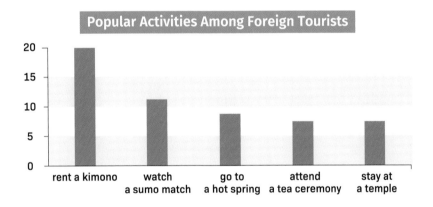

1. Why are kimonos popular among foreign tourists?

    _____.

2. What was the second most popular activity?

    _____.

3. Name one other activity unique to Japan.

    _____.

Let's Write ✏️

Choose an activity from the graph on page 27. Write about why you want to try it.

_____

_____

_____

Let's Talk 🔢 👥

Work in groups of three or more. Exchange ideas about Japanese activities you want to do with a friend from abroad. Tell the class about your group's discussion.

〈Example〉

In our group, all the students wanted to rent a kimono. We thought it would be exciting for friends from abroad to try on traditional Japanese clothes. We want to take many pictures with them.

📷 **What do you see?** Look at this photo and talk about it.

Part 2 | Was it difficult for you to explain it in English?

Let's Listen 🎧 ANSWER THE QUESTIONS

Rikuya is talking with Sayaka.

1. He joined ⬜ event.

   ☐ **(a)** an online

   ☐ **(b)** an outdoor

   ☐ **(c)** a sports

2. ☐ **(a)** A girl from Indonesia

   ☐ **(b)** A boy from Singapore

   ☐ **(c)** Aboriginal people from Australia

3. They ⬜ .

   ☐ **(a)** are curved wooden tools

   ☐ **(b)** are only used for playing tricks

   ☐ **(c)** come in different colors and shapes

Let's Read 1 📖 🔊

Rikuya: I joined an online event last weekend.

Sayaka: Cool! How was it?

Rikuya: Great. Students from around the world got together and shared their traditional cultures. I showed them how to play *kendama*.

Sayaka: Was it difficult for you to explain it in English?

Rikuya: Yes, but I showed them a trick, and everyone thought it was neat. A boy from Singapore introduced *Sepak Takraw*. It's a sport like volleyball, but you can only use your feet, knees, chest, and head to touch the ball.

Sayaka: Wow! Sounds really hard.

Rikuya: Yeah. An Indonesian girl performed a dance. She had on a traditional costume with beautiful colors.

Sayaka: That sounds interesting. What was your favorite?

Rikuya: The boomerang from Australia. It's a curved wooden tool that Aboriginal people use for hunting. Now, it's also used in a competitive sport.

Sayaka: I've seen boomerangs before. They come in different colors and shapes, don't they?

Rikuya: That's right. It looked like fun to throw and catch them outside.

Words & Phrases 🔊

neat 素敵な, すばらしい　　Sepak Takraw セパタクロー　　Indonesian インドネシア（人）の
boomerang ブーメラン　　curved 曲がった　　Aboriginal アボリジニ（オーストラリア先住民）の
competitive sport 競技

KEY PHRASES 🔊

Was it difficult for you to explain it in English?
They come in different colors and shapes, don't they?

Let's Practice 👥

Work in pairs and practice the conversation between Rikuya and Sayaka.
Change roles.

Let's Talk 1 💬

Work in pairs and talk about traditional Japanese cultures.
Change roles.

⟨ Example ⟩

A: I made sushi rolls last night.

B: That's great. Was it difficult for you to make?

A: [Yes, it was. My mother helped me. / No, it wasn't. I've done it before.

I'm used to cooking.]

A: Have you made an origami crane?

B: Yes.

A: Was it easy for you to make it?

B: [No, it wasn't. I'm not good at folding paper so perfectly. / Yes, I've

made it many times.]

Toolbox 🔊

弓道を体験する　try *kyudo*　　　　　凧揚げをする　fly a kite

羽根つきをする　play *hanetsuki*

Let's Read 2 📖 🔊

Read the webpage with the graph and answer the questions.

Welcome to the Global Student Program website. We have supported students wishing to study abroad for the past twenty years. This year, nearly two hundred students decided to study abroad through one of our programs. Most students participated in short programs during their spring, summer, or winter holidays. These programs range from two to four weeks, and about half of the students chose this option. Short programs are conducted in special classrooms just for international students. During the program, you will stay with a host family.

Some students have chosen to join longer programs that last more than seven months, because they were interested in attending regular classes in local schools. If you want to experience studying with other students in another country, we recommend this longer option.

The international experience will be something you will treasure for life. Improve your English skills and experience living in a different culture. The Global Student Program will help you step out into the world.

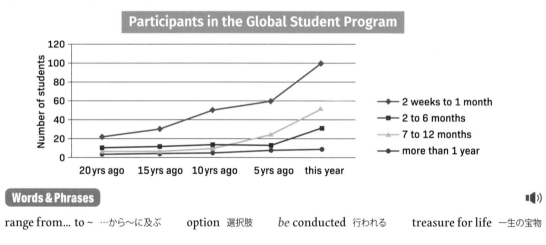

Participants in the Global Student Program

- 2 weeks to 1 month
- 2 to 6 months
- 7 to 12 months
- more than 1 year

Number of students (y-axis: 0, 20, 40, 60, 80, 100, 120)

20 yrs ago   15 yrs ago   10 yrs ago   5 yrs ago   this year

Words & Phrases 🔊

range from... to ~ …から~に及ぶ   option 選択肢   *be* conducted 行われる   treasure for life 一生の宝物

1. When do most students join short programs?

_____.

2. Are programs that last more than seven months the most popular option this year?

_____.

3. What can you experience through studying abroad?

_____.

Let's Write ✏️

You are going to study abroad and stay with a host family. Introduce some traditional Japanese culture to your host family. (Example: food, music, event)

_____

_____

_____

Let's Talk 2 💬

Work in groups of three or more. Exchange ideas about what traditional Japanese culture you want to introduce. Tell the class about your group's discussion.

〈Example〉

I'd like to talk about _____, because _____.

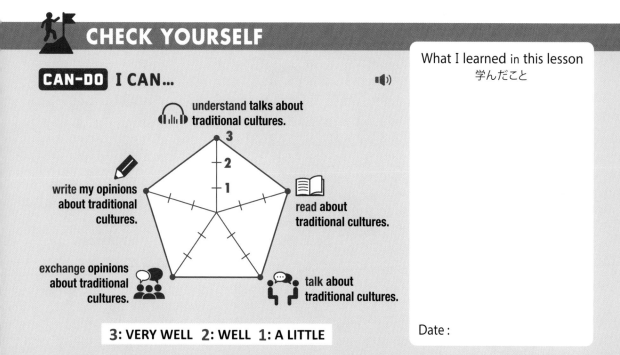

CHECK YOURSELF

CAN-DO I CAN... 🔊

- understand talks about traditional cultures.
- read about traditional cultures.
- talk about traditional cultures.
- exchange opinions about traditional cultures.
- write my opinions about traditional cultures.

3
2
1

3: VERY WELL 2: WELL 1: A LITTLE

What I learned in this lesson
学んだこと

Date :

PET BUSINESSES

CAN-DO

In this lesson, you will...

 listen **to talks** about pet businesses.

 read **about** pet businesses.

 talk **about** pet businesses.

 exchange **opinions** about pet businesses.

 write **your opinions** about pet businesses.

Part 1   What kind of animals do they sell?

Let's Listen 1 🎧 ANSWER THE QUESTIONS 🔊

Ken and Meg are talking.

1. It's near ☐ .

   ☐ (a) the school

   ☐ (b) the station

   ☐ (c) the shopping mall

2. ☐ (a) Unusual animals

   ☐ (b) Cute cats and dogs

   ☐ (c) Large fish and turtles

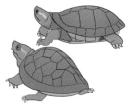

Let's Read 1

Ken: Hi, Meg. Did you notice the new pet shop?

Meg: The one near the station?

Ken: No. That's the old one.

Meg: Oh, where is the new pet shop?

Ken: It's near the shopping mall.

Meg: What kind of animals do they sell?

Ken: They sell unusual foreign animals.

Meg: Unusual foreign animals?

Ken: Yes. For example, colorful snakes, turtles, and beautiful tropical fish.

Meg: Sounds exciting. Do you think unusual pets will become popular in the future?

Ken: Yes, I think so.

Meg: Why?

Ken: Because many of them are very cute.

Words & Phrases

notice... …に気づく　　old one　古いもの（ここでは「前からあるペットショップ」のこと）　　kind of... …の種類

they sell... they は「店」のこと　　foreign animals　外来動物

KEY PHRASES

Do you think unusual pets will become popular in the future?

Yes, I think so.

No, I don't think so.

Let's Practice 1

Work in pairs and practice the conversation between Ken and Meg.
Change roles.

Let's Practice 2 👥

Work in pairs. Ask about pets and reply as in the example.
Change roles.

〈Example〉

> A: Do you think <u>cats</u> will become more popular in the future?
>
> B: [Yes, I think so. / No, I don't think so.]
>
> A: [Why? / Why not?]
>
> B: Because [they're cute. / they scratch things.]

| dogs | little birds | snakes | robot pets |

> Yes の理由例： easy to take care of / quiet / show their feelings / cute
>
> No の理由例： difficult to take care of / often noisy / expensive / dangerous

Let's Talk 1 💬

Work in pairs and talk about unusual pets.
Change roles.

〈Example〉

> A: Do you think unusual pets will become popular in the future?
>
> B: [Yes. / No.]
>
> A: [Why? / Why not?]
>
> B: I think unusual pets are _____.

Toolbox 🔊

安くなっている	becoming cheaper		
たいていとても高い	usually very expensive	かわいくて安全な	cute and safe
世話しやすい	easy to [take care of / look after]	ときどき危険な	sometimes dangerous
世話しにくい	difficult to [take care of / look after]		

Let's Listen 2 🎧 ANSWER THE QUESTIONS 🔊

Ken is talking to Ms. Mason, a pet shop owner.

1. ☐ (a) Cats and dogs

   ☐ (b) Foreign animals

   ☐ (c) Small animals

2. Because they are [　　　]

   ☐ (a) not expensive

   ☐ (b) more popular

   ☐ (c) easy to take care of

3. Because people [　　　]

   ☐ (a) like pets

   ☐ (b) can relax with them

   ☐ (c) want to play with them

Let's Read 2 📖

Read the passage with the graph and answer the questions.

The number of pet shops in Greentown has changed in the past four years. Three years ago, not many people bought pets. After that, new pet shops opened because unusual pets from foreign countries became popular. However, these foreign animals are sometimes difficult to take care of. Some bad owners get rid of their pets by throwing them in rivers or leaving them in mountains. Some foreign animals attack local animals in Greentown, and this is a serious problem now.

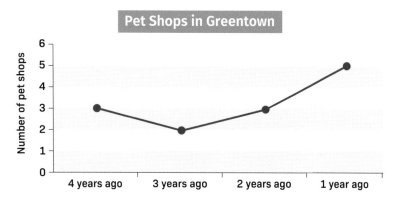

Pet Shops in Greentown

Words & Phrases

have changed 変化してきた　　in the past four years 過去4年間で　　local animals 在来動物

get rid of... …を捨てる

1. How many pet shops were there three years ago?

_____.

2. Why did the number of pet shops start to go up two years ago?

_____.

3. Why do some pet owners of foreign animals get rid of their pets?

_____.

4. What is a big problem now in Greentown?

_____.

Let's Write ✏

Do you think there will be more pet shops in the future? Why or why not?

_____

_____

_____

Let's Talk 2 💬

Work in groups of three or more. Exchange ideas about pet shops in the future. Tell the class about your group's discussion.

〈 Example 〉

In our group, many students think the number of pet shops will ［ go up / go down ］ in the

future. The main reason is that _____ .

📷 What do you see?   Look at this photo and talk about it.

Part **2**   **I'm worried about my dog.**

Let's Listen 🎧 ANSWER THE QUESTIONS 🔊

Ayame and Jon are talking.

1. He ☐ .

　　☐ (a) is very noisy

　　☐ (b) eats too much

　　☐ (c) looks very tired

2. It's ☐ .

　　☐ (a) near the station

　　☐ (b) next to the school

　　☐ (c) in the shopping mall

3. Her parents ☐ .

　　☐ (a) live near it

　　☐ (b) saw it last week

　　☐ (c) went there last year

Let's Read 1 📖 🔊

Ayame: Are you OK, Jon? You look worried.

Jon: I am. I'm worried about my dog.

Ayame: What's the problem with your dog?

Jon: He doesn't eat much and looks very tired.

Ayame: I see. You should take him to a vet. There is a good animal hospital near the station.

Jon: Really? How do you know the hospital?

Ayame: Last year, my cat was very sick, and my parents took her there. The vet was very kind and good.

Jon: I see. I'll talk to my parents. Thanks for the advice.

Ayame: Not at all.

Words & Phrases 🔊

look worried 不安そうな顔をしている   *be* worried about... …を心配している   take ~ to... ～を…へ連れて行く

Not at all. どういたしまして。   vet（veterinarian）獣医

KEY PHRASES 🔊

What's the problem with your dog?

He doesn't eat much and looks very tired.

Let's Practice

Work in pairs and practice the conversation between Ayame and Jon.
Change roles.

Let's Talk **1**

**Work in pairs. Choose a pet from the pictures and talk about it.
Change roles.**

〈 Example 〉

> A: Are you OK, (NAME)? You look worried.
>
> B: I am. I'm worried about my [   ].
>
> A: What's the problem with your 【(pet)】?
>
> B: [He / She / It] _____.
>
> A: You should take [him / her / it] to an animal hospital.
>
> B: Thanks for the advice.

【pet】

others

Toolbox [problems with your pet]

あまり食べない	doesn't eat much
[やせて／毛が抜けて／羽が抜けて]きた	is losing [weight / fur / feathers]
太ってきた	is gaining weight
くさい, 変なにおいがする	smells bad
吠えすぎる	barks too often
しばしば人にかみつく	often bites people
しばしば私の腕をひっかく	often scratches my arm
皮膚に赤い斑点がある	has red spots on the skin

Let's Read 2 📖 🔊

Read the passage with the graph and answer the questions.

People take their pets to animal hospitals for different reasons. There are many kinds of pets, and vets are becoming very busy. Because the treatments for pets are usually expensive, some pet owners do not take their pets to the hospital. This can be a big problem for their pets. These days, there are many kinds of pet insurance for cats and dogs, and they can help pet owners pay for the treatments.

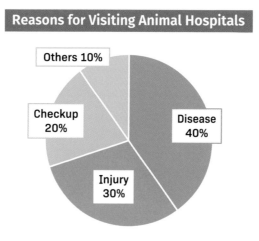

Reasons for Visiting Animal Hospitals

Others 10%
Checkup 20%
Disease 40%
Injury 30%

Words & Phrases 🔊

treatments 治療　　pet insurance ペット保険　　injury ケガ　　checkup 健康診断
pay for... …を支払う　　*the second biggest 2番目に大きな

1. What is *the second biggest reason for visiting animal hospitals?

_____ .

2. Why are vets becoming very busy?

_____ .

3. What can help pet owners pay for the treatments?

_____ .

Let's Write ✏️

Do you think there will be more animal hospitals in the future? Why or why not?

_____

_____

_____

Let's Talk 2 💬

Work in groups of three or more. Exchange ideas about animal hospitals. Tell the class about your group's discussion.

〈 Example 〉

In our group, more students think the number of animal hospitals 〔 will go up / will not go up 〕 in the future. The main reason is that _____.

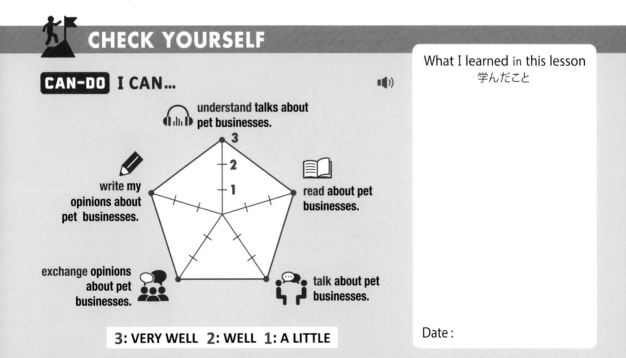

CHECK YOURSELF

CAN-DO I CAN... 🔊

- understand **talks about pet businesses.**
- read **about pet businesses.**
- talk **about pet businesses.**
- exchange **opinions about pet businesses.**
- write **my opinions about pet businesses.**

3: VERY WELL 2: WELL 1: A LITTLE

What I learned in this lesson
学んだこと

Date :

Lesson 4
FAVORITE BOOKS & MAGAZINES

CAN-DO

In this lesson, you will...

 listen **to talks** about books and magazines. read **about books** and magazines.

 talk **about books** and magazines. exchange **opinions** about books and magazines. write **your opinions** about books and magazines.

Part 1   I didn't know that you're an anime fan.

Let's Listen 1   ANSWER THE QUESTIONS

Meg is talking with her father Tony.

1. ☐ (a) Meg

    ☐ (b) Yumi

    ☐ (c) Tony

2. Because the anime stories ☐

    ☐ (a) are always very interesting

    ☐ (b) are helpful in many ways

    ☐ (c) look the same to Tony

Let's Read 1 📖 🔊

Tony: Hi, Meg. What's up?

Meg: Hi, Dad. I just borrowed this magazine from Yumi.

Tony: May I take a look?

Meg: Sure. It's a special issue of the 30 Best Anime Series in the world this year.

Tony: I didn't know that you're an anime fan.

Meg: Not really. But Yumi is.

Tony: I see. Many of the characters in this magazine look the same to me.

Meg: Oh, no, Dad. The anime stories are very interesting. Try reading my favorite anime series, and you'll see the differences.

Tony: Thank you, Meg, but maybe some other time. I like reading books better. I enjoy books and sometimes find them really useful.

Words & Phrases 🔊

borrow　借りる　　special issue　特別号　　the 30 Best Anime Series　アニメ作品ベスト30

maybe some other time　また別の機会に

KEY PHRASES 🔊

I didn't know that you're a big anime fan.

Thank you,（Meg,）but maybe some other time.

Let's Practice 1 👥

**Work in pairs and practice the conversation between Tony and Meg.
Change roles.**

Let's Practice 2

Work in pairs. Ask about your partner's favorite and reply as in the example.
Change roles.

〈Example〉

A: Are you a/an 【 ① 】 fan?

B: Yes, I am. I like it very much. It's very 【 ② 】.

A: Are you a/an 【 ① 】 fan?

B: No, not really. I like 【 ③ 】 better. They're very 【 ② 】.

①③	anime / manga / movie / TV drama / music / sports
②	interesting / funny / useful / helpful / exciting / informative / humorous / relaxing / beautiful / enjoyable

Let's Talk 1

Work in pairs and talk about manga and books.
Change roles.

〈Example〉

A: Which do you like better, manga or books?

B: I _____.

A: Why?

B: Because _____.

Toolbox

わくわくする	exciting
おもしろい	funny
役に立つ	useful
気軽に読める	easy to read
［マンガ／本］の世界に入りこめる	can get into the world of ［manga / books］

Let's Listen ❷ 🎧 ANSWER THE QUESTIONS 🔊

Ken and Ms. Mason are talking.

1. Ken wanted ☐ .

    ☐ (a) to thank her for the book she lent him the other day

    ☐ (b) to ask her a few more questions about pets

    ☐ (c) to buy a book on unusual pets

2. He is ☐ .

    ☐ (a) curious about unusual pet animals

    ☐ (b) happy to meet Ms. Mason after a long time

    ☐ (c) hoping to order a pet magazine from abroad

Let's Read 2 📖 🔊

Read the passage and answer the questions.

There's a brand-new library downtown. It's the place for information and learning for everyone in town.

On the first floor, there's a big general reading area. It's divided into three zones: (1) books and reference zone, (2) newspapers, magazines, and comic books zone, (3) audio-visual and ICT zone.

The whole second floor is a unique zone called U-18. The U-18 zone has been prepared for school children, junior and senior high school students, and teachers. This is very unique. There are two classrooms, five smaller rooms, ten individual booths with computers, and 20 comfortable chairs to enjoy reading books and magazines.

The library is open every day between 8 a.m. and 6 p.m., except between December 30 and January 3.

Words & Phrases 🔊

brand-new 真新しい   learning 学習   general 通常の   zone 区域   reference 参考文献

audio-visual 視聴覚の   ICT = Information and Communication Technology 情報通信技術

whole 全体の   U-18 = under 18 18歳以下   *be* prepared 用意された   individual 個別の

comfortable 快適な   except... …以外

1. What is the purpose of the new library?

_____.

2. Where should parents go when they want to search the internet at the library?

_____.

3. What is unique about the new library?

_____.

Let's Write ✎

What kind of library do you want to have at your school? Draw your floor plan and explain it.

Let's Talk ❷

Work in groups of three or more. Exchange ideas about your ideal school library. Tell the class about your group's discussion.

📷 **What do you see?** Look at this photo and talk about it.

Part 2

All you have to do is read the poem aloud over and over again.

Let's Listen 🎧 ANSWER THE QUESTIONS 🔊

Hayato and Ms. Kimura are talking.

1. Because Hayato ☐☐☐☐

    ☐ (a) is not ready for his presentation

    ☐ (b) is not good at reading aloud

    ☐ (c) has chosen a short story

2. ☐ (a) The shorter, the better.

    ☐ (b) Don't change your mind.

    ☐ (c) It's not that easy.

Let's Read 1 📖

🔊

Hayato:	Hi, Ms. Kimura.
Ms. Kimura:	Hi, Hayato. You look worried. Are you OK?
Hayato:	Oh, I'm fine, but I'm not quite ready for my presentation next week.
Ms. Kimura:	You mean Mr. King's assignment?
Hayato:	Yes, that's right. We're expected to choose one short story or a poem from his list, and make a short presentation in class.
Ms. Kimura:	I heard. Have you picked a story or a poem yet?
Hayato:	Yes, I've chosen one poem. I first thought, "The shorter, the easier."
Ms. Kimura:	I know what you mean. But it wasn't that easy, right?
Hayato:	Now I'm thinking about changing it to a short story.
Ms. Kimura:	Well, you've already spent some time on the poem, so go with your choice.
Hayato:	I'm not sure.
Ms. Kimura:	All you have to do is read the poem aloud over and over again, until you know it by heart. Then you'll naturally see the answer.

Words & Phrases 🔊

poem 詩　　the shorter, the easier 短いほど簡単　　I know what you mean. なるほど。
go with... …をやり通す　　All you have to do is.... …しさえすればいい。　　over and over again 何度も何度も
know it by heart 暗記する

Let's Practice

Work in pairs and practice the conversation between Hayato and Ms. Kimura.
Change roles.

Let's Talk 1

Work in pairs. Talk about a presentation you're going to make about a short story, a poem, or another kind of art.
Change roles.

〈 Example 〉

A: What do you want to choose for your presentation?

B: I want to speak about [a short story / a poem].

A: Why?

B: Because _____ .

How about you?

A: _____ .

Toolbox

マンガ	manga	おもしろい	interesting / funny
雑誌	a magazine	美しい	beautiful
絵本	a picture book	心温まる	heart-warming
映画	a movie	得るものが大きい	informative
テレビ番組	a TV program	感動的な	moving
歌	a song	印象深い	impressive
絵	a painting	深い意味がある	have a deep meaning
		たくさん考えさせる	make me think a lot

Let's Read 2 📖 🔊

Read the passage and answer the questions.

How do you find the book that you want to buy at a bookstore, or borrow from your school library? The easiest way is to ask a clerk or a librarian to see if they have the book and where you can find it. Or there may be a computer to assist you in finding the book, and needless to say, you must use a digital device to search an e-book catalog.

Below are two sets of completely different categories, or subject matter (Table A and Table B) for the library.

Table A	
General Works	総記
Philosophy	哲学
History	歴史
Social Sciences	社会科学
Natural Sciences	自然科学
Technology & Engineering	技術
Industry & Commerce	産業
Arts	芸術
Language	言語
Literature	文学

Table B	
Realistic Fiction	写実小説
Historical Fiction	歴史小説
Traditional Literature	伝統文学
Science Fiction	空想科学小説
Fantasy	空想小説
Mystery	推理小説
Informational	情報提供型
Biography	伝記
Autobiography	自叙伝
Poetry	詩歌

Which list is more helpful and interesting to you? Table A may be much more familiar because it's based on the Japanese school library catalog system. Table B may look like a list for children, and the category "Informational" seems to cover many of the categories in Table A.

It's very important to know the kind of catalog system your library has. Can you tell where you could find your favorite book in both of these systems?

Words & Phrases 🔊

clerk 係の人　　needless to say 言うまでもなく　　digital device デジタル機器　　e-book 電子書籍

category 範疇（はんちゅう）　　subject matter 主題　　catalog system 分類方式

1. How do you find the book that you want to buy at a bookstore?

_____.

2. Where would you find books on "traditional music in Okinawa" in both systems?

_____.

3. Which system would be more useful to a junior high school student?

_____.

Let's Write ✏️

How would you want to make better use of your school library? What kind of books, magazines, and other services would you want to include?

_____

_____

_____

Let's Talk 2

Work in groups of three or more. Exchange ideas about books, magazines, or anything that you want to add to your school library. Tell the class about your group's discussion.

〈 Example 〉

In our group, everyone wants the library to have many individual booths with computers.

One student wants the library to stay open until 7 p.m. when big tests are scheduled.

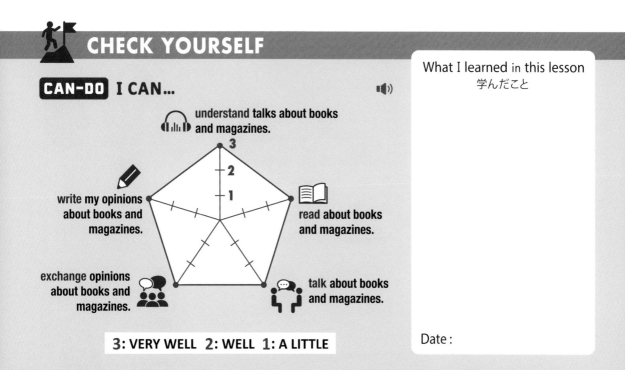

CHECK YOURSELF

CAN-DO **I CAN...** 🔊

What I learned in this lesson
学んだこと

understand **talks about books** and magazines.

3
2
1

write my opinions about books and magazines.

read **about books** and magazines.

exchange **opinions** about books and magazines.

talk **about books** and magazines.

3: VERY WELL 2: WELL 1: A LITTLE

Date :

TAKING A TRIP

CAN-DO

In this lesson, you will...

 listen to talks about traveling.

> read about traveling.

> talk about traveling.

> exchange opinions about traveling.

> write your opinions about traveling.

Part 1 Could you make the reservation for me?

Let's Listen 1 ANSWER THE QUESTIONS

Mr. King is talking with a clerk at a travel agency.

1. He wants to go to Hokkaido ☐ .

    ☐ **(a)** to meet his old friends

    ☐ **(b)** to see the Sapporo Snow Festival

    ☐ **(c)** to travel with his father

2. He has to ☐ at the agency.

    ☐ **(a)** pay some money

    ☐ **(b)** reserve hotels

    ☐ **(c)** show his passport

Let's Read 1 📖 🔊

Mr. King: Do you have package tours for older people?

Clerk: Yes, we do. When, where to, and for how long?

Mr. King: We, I mean my father and I, would like to travel in Hokkaido next summer. We want to go for four or five days. He's coming to Japan, and I'm going to show him around Hokkaido.

Clerk: Let me see. How about this 5-day, 4-night package tour? You stay in one place a day, and only the time to move to the next place is fixed. You can also choose hotels. It's very popular. So, if you like it, you can reserve hotels now and finish your application.

Mr. King: Hmm. OK. Which hotels are available?

Clerk: Here's the list. Let me bring you their brochures.

Words & Phrases 🔊

package tour パッケージ旅行　　I mean... つまり…　　show... around …を案内してまわる

let me see 少しお待ちください　　fixed 定まっている　　reserve 予約する　　application 申し込み

available 利用できる　　brochure 案内パンフレット

KEY PHRASE 🔊

Let me bring you their brochures.

Let's Practice 1 👥

Work in pairs and practice the conversation between Mr. King and the clerk.
Change roles.

Let's Practice ❷ 👥

Work in pairs. Ask about means of traveling and reply as in the example. Change roles.

〈 Example 〉

> A: How do you want to go to Hokkaido?
>
> B: I'd like to go there by [plane / train / ferry].
>
> A: Then, let me reserve it for you. How about the hotel?
>
> B: I'll reserve the hotel myself.

Let's Talk ❶ 💬

Work in pairs and talk about your trip. Choose three or more questions from A1–A5. Change roles.

〈 Example 〉

Ⓐ 1. Where do you want to go? ➡ Ⓑ I want to go to _____.

    2. How do you want to go there? ➡ I want to go there by _____.

    3. How long do you want to stay there? ➡ I want to stay there for _____ days.

    4. Who will go with you? ➡ _____ will go with me.

    5. What do you want to do there? ➡ I want to _____.

Ⓐ Do you have any other requests?

Ⓑ No. That's all.

Ⓐ Then, you should (not) [take a package tour. /
other suggestions: _____.]

Toolbox 🔊

買い物に行く
  go shopping

サイクリングをする
  go cycling

ハイキングに行く
  go hiking

地元の料理を食べる
  eat the local dishes

農場で働く
  work on a farm

親戚／名所を訪ねる
  visit [relatives / famous places]

Let's Listen 2 🎧 ANSWER THE QUESTIONS 🔊

Ms. Mori is talking with a clerk at a travel agency.

1. ☐ (a) During the summer vacation

   ☐ (b) Next month

   ☐ (c) When it's not hot

2. ☐ (a) In Tokyo

   ☐ (b) In Kyoto

   ☐ (c) In Nara

Let's Read 2 📖 🔊

Read the passage with the graph and answer the questions.

If you want to experience the atmosphere of traditional Japan, I recommend Kyoto and Nara first. Of course, they are modern cities now but are still full of historical attractions. You should stay at a traditional inn and discover the cities yourself — buildings, gardens, food, hospitality, and more. To get around, you can use public transportation such as trains and buses. However, if you stay there for two or more nights, I strongly recommend using a bike on one of those days. Walking is another good choice, but you can get around much faster and more easily by bike, especially in those compact cities. You will be able to discover a lot of exciting and interesting things on your own. Keep your fingers crossed for days without rain or snow.

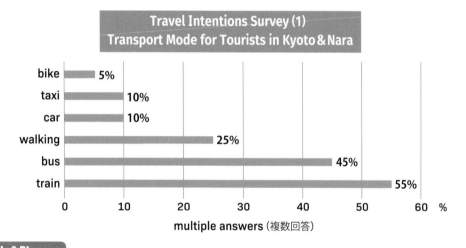

Travel Intentions Survey (1)
Transport Mode for Tourists in Kyoto & Nara

bike 5%
taxi 10%
car 10%
walking 25%
bus 45%
train 55%

multiple answers (複数回答)

Words & Phrases 🔊

atmosphere 雰囲気   discover 見つけ出す   hospitality もてなし方   public 公共の
transportation 交通機関   on *one's* own 自分一人で   keep *one's* fingers crossed 幸運を祈る

1. What is the most popular means of transportation when moving around cities like Kyoto or Nara?

_____.

2. Why is walking or cycling recommended to tourists in Kyoto or Nara?

_____.

3. Do you think the weather changes one's choice of transportation?

_____.

Let's Write ✏️

Write about your plan for a short trip.

_____

_____

_____

Let's Talk 2 💬👥

Work in groups of three or more and talk about what you wrote above. Tell the class about your group's discussion.

📷 What do you see? Look at this photo and talk about it.

Part 2 Don't you know their itinerary?

Let's Listen 🎧 ANSWER THE QUESTIONS 🔊

Rikuya and Sayaka are talking.

1. They like to travel ⬚ .

    ☐ (a) alone

    ☐ (b) on a package tour

    ☐ (c) without a detailed itinerary

2. Because he got ⬚ from them yesterday

    ☐ (a) a phone call

    ☐ (b) a letter

    ☐ (c) a text message

Let's Read 1

Rikuya: My grandparents are traveling abroad now. They left Japan two weeks ago. They texted us last night for the first time, and said they are staying at a hotel on the West Coast now.

Sayaka: Don't you know their itinerary?

Rikuya: No. They always like traveling without a detailed itinerary.

Sayaka: It seems they like traveling itself, not necessarily the destinations.

Rikuya: Maybe. Don't you know their itinerary? It took such a long time to get there. They're so unpredictable.

Sayaka: Oh, but I think it's nice. I'd like to take the same kind of trip myself someday.

Words & Phrases

text... …にメールを送る　　the West Coast アメリカ西海岸　　itinerary 旅行計画　　detailed 詳しい

not necessarily 必ずしも…でない　　destinations 目的地　　unpredictable 行動が読めない

KEY PHRASE

It seems they like traveling itself.

Let's Practice

Work in pairs and practice the conversation between Rikuya and Sayaka.
Change roles.

Let's Talk 1

Work in pairs and share your opinion about traveling.
Change roles.

〈 Example 〉

A
- What kind of transportation do you want to use?
- Where do you want to go?
- What kind of activity do you want to do at your destination?
- Who do you want to go with?

B　I want to go ＿＿＿＿＿＿＿＿. ＿＿＿＿＿＿＿＿. (*Comment*)

A　How about ＿＿＿＿＿＿＿＿? (*Another idea on the same topic*)

B　That's a good idea, too. / I'm not ＿＿＿＿＿＿＿＿＿＿＿＿.
　　＿＿＿＿＿＿＿＿＿＿＿＿＿＿＿＿＿＿. (*Comment*)

Let's Read 2 📖 🔊

Read the passage with the graph and answer the questions.

I like traveling alone by planning everything on my own. I think there are four stages in a trip.

The first stage is preparation. It includes creating an itinerary and making bookings, packing my backpack, and trying to find the best ways to enjoy the trip.

The second is the journey on a train, bus, ship, or plane. On the way, I can meet new people, see beautiful scenery, and enjoy the time while traveling.

The trip's highlights come when I spend time at the destination. I visit the places I planned and do what I can't do normally. I can enjoy the local food, stay overnight at an inn, talk with other guests, and broaden my knowledge and experiences.

The final stage is the way back home. It may be a sad stage for some people, but I like it, too. I look back on the journey before I get home, and I feel, "I did it."

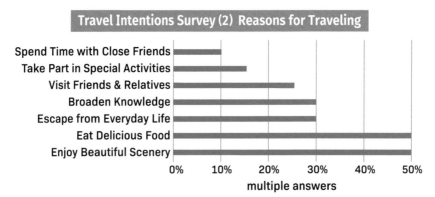

Travel Intentions Survey (2) Reasons for Traveling

alone ひとりで   stage 段階   preparation 準備   journey 旅, 行程   scenery 景色, 風景

broaden 広める   look back on... …を振り返る   close friends 親しい友達   take part in... …に参加する

escape from... …から脱出する   everyday 普段の

1. What does the writer of the passage do on the way home?

_____ .

2. What are the purposes in the graph that are NOT mentioned in the passage?

_____ .

3. What purpose of traveling is as important as broadening one's knowledge?

_____ .

Let's Write ✏️

What do you think you would enjoy the most when traveling? Write your opinion with examples.

_____

_____

_____

Let's Talk 2 🗣️

Work in groups of three or more. Exchange ideas about the main purposes of taking a trip. Tell the class about your group's discussion.

〈 Example 〉

[Your Friend's Name] wants _____.

_____. (*Comment*)

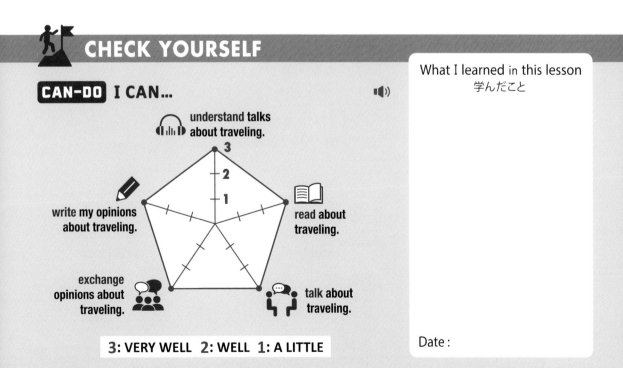

CHECK YOURSELF

CAN-DO I CAN... 🔊

- 🎧 understand talks about traveling.
- 📖 read about traveling.
- 🗣️ talk about traveling.
- 🗣️ exchange opinions about traveling.
- ✏️ write my opinions about traveling.

3: VERY WELL 2: WELL 1: A LITTLE

What I learned in this lesson
学んだこと

Date :

Lesson 6
FOOD WASTE

CAN-DO

In this lesson,
you will...

 listen to talks
about food
problems.

 read about
food problems.

 talk about
food problems.

 exchange opinions
about food
problems.

 write your opinions
about food
problems.

Part **1** What do you do when something you don't like is served?

Let's Listen **1** 🎧 ANSWER THE QUESTIONS

Ayame and Hayato are talking.

1. He doesn't like food seasoned with ☐ .

   ☐ (a) coriander

   ☐ (b) garlic

   ☐ (c) ketchup

2. ☐ (a) He eats it.

   ☐ (b) He leaves it.

   ☐ (c) He takes it home.

Let's Read 1 ◄))

Ayame: Is there any food you don't like?

Hayato: Yes. I don't like natto or raw eggs, and I don't like food seasoned
         with coriander.

Ayame: I see. What do you do when such food is served?

Hayato: I won't eat it. I'll just leave it.

Ayame: What if a meal consists of all the things you don't like to eat?

Hayato: Hmm. If I am very hungry and nothing else is available, I will
         probably eat them.

Words & Phrases ◄))

raw eggs 生卵   seasoned with... …で味をつけた   coriander コリアンダー（パクチー）

be served 出される   What if...? もし…だったらどうするの。

KEY PHRASES

... when such food is served

If I am very hungry and nothing else is available,...

Let's Practice 1

**Work in pairs and practice the conversation between Ayame and Hayato.
Change roles.**

What do you see?

Look at this photo and
talk about it.

Let's Practice ❷ 👥

Work in pairs. Ask about seasonings and reply as in the example.
Change roles.

〈Example〉

1. Ⓐ Do you like food seasoned with [   ]?
coriander / garlic / ginger / ketchup / miso / soy sauce / vinegar /
(other seasonings:)
Ⓑ Yes, I do.
Ⓐ If someone serves it to you, what will you say?
Ⓑ I will say, "_____."

2. Ⓐ Do you like food seasoned with [   ]?
Ⓑ No, I don't.
Ⓐ If a meal consists of all the things you don't like to eat, what will you do?
Ⓑ I'll _____.

3. Ⓐ Do you like food seasoned with [   ]?
Ⓑ It's OK.
Ⓐ What is your favorite seasoning?
Ⓑ I like food seasoned with _____.

Let's Talk ❶ 💬

Work in pairs and talk about what you do when something you don't like is served.
Change roles.

〈Example〉

A: What do you do when something you don't like is served?

B: Well, I'll _____ if _____. What do you do?

A: I'll _____ if _____.

Toolbox 🔊

全部食べるようにがんばる	try to eat it all
何か口実をつけて残す	leave it on my plate with some excuse
食事に招かれている	*be* invited for dinner
おごってもらっている	*be* treated

Let's Listen 2 ANSWER THE QUESTIONS

Rikuya and Ayame are talking.

1. He went to [   ] .

☐ (a) a Thai restaurant

☐ (b) Ayame's house

☐ (c) his Thai friend's house

2. Because [   ]

☐ (a) he thought about the food waste campaign

☐ (b) he was very hungry

☐ (c) they were hot but tasty

Let's Read **2** 📖

Read the passage with the graph and answer the questions.

This year our student council has taken up the problem of food waste. They surveyed all the students and got the following results. They noticed some interesting relationships among their eating habits, knowledge about food waste, and table manners.

Most of the students who answered [B] or [C] understood and showed concern about the food waste problem, while those who answered [A] knew little about it or were not interested. All the students who answered "Normally" in [C] said they were always told at home not to leave anything on their plates.

The student council discussed the findings and they concluded that the first thing is to let everyone at school know about the problem of food waste. So now, they are preparing a campaign against leftovers at the school cafeteria, with the slogan "Food Waste: Think Globally, Act Locally."

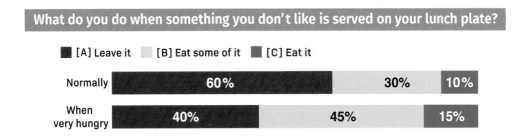

What do you do when something you don't like is served on your lunch plate?

■ [A] Leave it   [B] Eat some of it   ■ [C] Eat it

	[A] Leave it	[B] Eat some of it	[C] Eat it
Normally	60%	30%	10%
When very hungry	40%	45%	15%

Words & Phrases

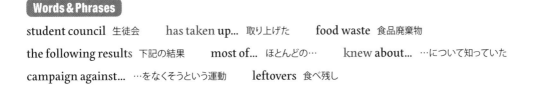

student council 生徒会   has taken up... 取り上げた   food waste 食品廃棄物

the following results 下記の結果   most of... ほとんどの…   knew about... …について知っていた

campaign against... …をなくそうという運動   leftovers 食べ残し

1. What do most students normally do when something they don't like is served?

_____.

2. Why did the student council do a survey of all the students?

_____.

3. What do you think the graph tells us?

_____.

Let's Write ✏️

Write your opinion about what we should do when something we don't like is served.

_____

_____

_____

Let's Talk 2 💬

Work in groups of three or more. Share your experience at the table when something you don't like is served. Tell the class about your group's discussion.

📷 **What do you see?** Look at this map and talk about it.

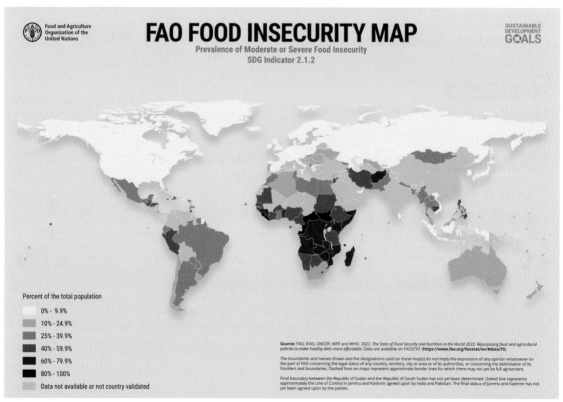

Food and Agriculture Organization of the United Nations

FAO FOOD INSECURITY MAP
Prevalence of Moderate or Severe Food Insecurity
SDG Indicator 2.1.2

SUSTAINABLE DEVELOPMENT GOALS

Percent of the total population

- 0% - 9.9%
- 10% - 24.9%
- 25% - 39.9%
- 40% - 59.9%
- 60% - 79.9%
- 80% - 100%
- Data not available or not country validated

Source: FAO, IFAD, UNICEF, WFP and WHO. 2022. *The State of Food Security and Nutrition in the World 2022. Repurposing food and agricultural policies to make healthy diets more affordable.* Data are available on FAOSTAT (https://www.fao.org/faostat/en/#data/FS)

The boundaries and names shown and the designations used on these map(s) do not imply the expression of any opinion whatsoever on the part of FAO concerning the legal status of any country, territory, city or area or of its authorities, or concerning the delimitation of its frontiers and boundaries. Dashed lines on maps represent approximate border lines for which there may not yet be full agreement.

Final boundary between the Republic of Sudan and the Republic of South Sudan has not yet been determined. Dotted line represents approximately the Line of Control in Jammu and Kashmir agreed upon by India and Pakistan. The final status of Jammu and Kashmir has not yet been agreed upon by the parties.

出典　国際連合食糧農業機関（FAO）

Part 2
Do you know how much food is thrown away every day?

Let's Listen ANSWER THE QUESTIONS

Rikuya and Ayame are talking.

1. They are talking about ☐.

   ☐ **(a)** buying food past their best-before date

   ☐ **(b)** food that is thrown away every day

   ☐ **(c)** small children who can't get enough food

2. They think ☐ is the best way to solve the problem.

   ☐ **(a)** buying just enough food and eating it up

   ☐ **(b)** reducing the number of meals a day

   ☐ **(c)** collecting as many food leftovers as possible

Let's Read **1** 📖 🔊

Rikuya: Do you know how much food is thrown away every day?

Ayame: Yes. I was shocked to hear that food leftovers and food past their best-before date are just thrown away in landfills.

Rikuya: I really think we should think about the people who can't get enough food in the world.

Ayame: Yes, I agree.

Rikuya: Buying just enough food and eating it up is probably the best way to reduce food waste.

Ayame: That's just what I was thinking.

Words & Phrases 🔊

be thrown away 捨てられる   *be* shocked to... …してショックを受ける   past... …を過ぎた

best-before date 賞味期限の日付   landfills ごみ埋め立て地   agree（with...） （…に）賛成である

KEY PHRASES 🔊

Yes, I agree.

That's just what I was thinking.

Let's Practice

Work in pairs and practice the conversation between Rikuya and Ayame. Change roles.

Let's Talk 1

Work in pairs and share your ideas about reducing food waste.
Change roles.

〈 Example 〉

> A: What do you think we should do when we can choose what we are
>
> going to eat?
>
> B: I think we should（not）[buy / take / order / use / .....] _____.
>
> A: I see. What about when the dishes are already in front of you?
>
> B: I think we should（not）[eat / touch / .....] _____.

Toolbox

丁度自分が食べられる量	just as much as we can eat
食べたくないもの	what we don't want to eat
好きでないものが付け合わせになっている料理	dishes with something we don't like
できるだけたくさん	as much as we can
その棚の食品を先に食べる	eat food from that shelf first

Let's Read 2 📖 🔊

Read the passage with the graph and answer the questions.

Many people have now realized how much food we throw away every day and are thinking seriously about solving this problem. Here's how one small city in Japan tackles this issue.

Plastics, paper, glass, and clothes, are collected once a week. However, new unused food and leftovers are collected daily to use as livestock food while "fresh." For this purpose, people have to separate still edible leftovers and uneaten food past its best-before date, and then put them out separately in a special box.

What is not suitable as livestock food is used to make compost, and produce energy. The city recommends using doggy bags or bringing a container from home when eating out. They also encourage collaborations in creating and supporting food banks and food bank networks.

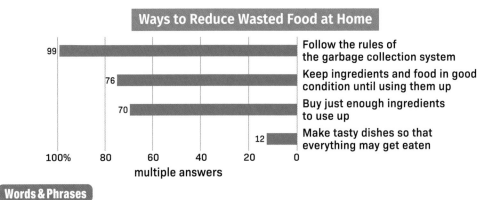

Ways to Reduce Wasted Food at Home

Value	Description
99	Follow the rules of the garbage collection system
76	Keep ingredients and food in good condition until using them up
70	Buy just enough ingredients to use up
12	Make tasty dishes so that everything may get eaten

100% 80 60 40 20 0
multiple answers

Words & Phrases 🔊

tackle... …に取り組む   *be* collected 回収される   livestock food 家畜の餌   separate 分ける, 分別する

still edible まだ食べられる   suitable 適した   compost 堆肥   doggy bag 持ち帰り袋

container 容器, 入れもの   eat out 外食する   encourage collaborations 協力を奨励する   support 支援する

1. What do people in the city have to do before they throw away food past its best-before date and still edible leftovers?

_____.

2. What is the percentage of the families in the city who buy just enough ingredients to use up?

_____.

3. Do you think the garbage collecting system in the city is working well? Why or why not?

_____.

Let's Write ✏️

Write about what you think we should do to reduce food waste.

_____

_____

_____

Let's Talk 2 🗨️

Work in groups of three or more. Exchange ideas about what you can do to reduce food waste. Tell the class about your group's discussion.

〈Example〉

_____ thinks that _____ . I think _____ .

_____ . 〈Comment〉

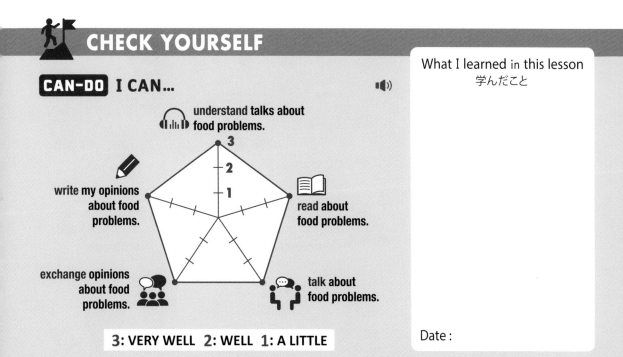

🚩 CHECK YOURSELF

CAN-DO I CAN... 🔊

understand talks about food problems.

write my opinions about food problems.

read about food problems.

exchange opinions about food problems.

talk about food problems.

3: VERY WELL   2: WELL   1: A LITTLE

What I learned in this lesson
学んだこと

Date :

Lesson 7
GARBAGE PROBLEMS

CAN-DO

In this lesson, you will...

 listen to talks about garbage problems.

 read about garbage problems.

 talk about garbage problems.

 exchange opinions about garbage problems.

 write your opinions about garbage problems.

Part 1 It will help reduce garbage from home.

Let's Listen 1 🎧 ANSWER THE QUESTIONS 🔊

Jon and Yumi are talking.

1. Yumi used the yarns that ☐☐☐ .

    ☐ (a) her grandma bought her

    ☐ (b) she collected at her school

    ☐ (c) she took from her family's old sweaters

2. Because Yumi ☐☐☐

    ☐ (a) and her grandma came up with the idea

    ☐ (b) learned how to knit at school

    ☐ (c) wanted to recycle used sweaters

Let's Read 1 📖 🔊

Jon: Yumi, you are wearing a nice sweater. It looks good on you and very original.

Yumi: Thank you, Jon. I'll tell you why this looks so original.

Jon: Tell me. What's different about it?

Yumi: I didn't use new yarn for this sweater. Well, I bought some red yarn, but I took more than 80% of the yarn from my family's used sweaters.

Jon: Wow, you knitted it by yourself?

Yumi: My grandma helped me. Remember we learned garbage is one of the most serious problems today?

Jon: Yes, we talked about how to reduce garbage. Is that the reason why you knitted it with old yarn?

Yumi: Yes, if we use used yarn, it will help reduce garbage from home.

Jon: What's more, it is very stylish and unique.

Yumi: I believe we can come up with many other good ideas to reduce garbage.

Words & Phrases 🔊

sweater セーター   look good on... （服などが）…に似合う   original 個性がある   yarn 毛糸
used 使用済みの   knit-knitted 編む   by *oneself* 一人で   stylish かっこいい   come up with 思いつく

KEY PHRASES 🔊

We talked about how to reduce garbage.
If we use used yarns again, it will help reduce garbage from home.

Let's Practice 1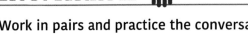

Work in pairs and practice the conversation between Jon and Yumi.
Change roles.

Let's Practice 2 👥

Work in pairs. Practice the conversation as in the example.
Change roles.

〈 Example 〉

> A: We talked about how to reduce 【 ① 】.
>
> B: If we 【 ② 】, it will help reduce 【 ① 】.

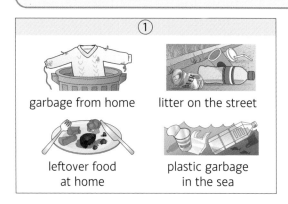

① garbage from home | litter on the street | leftover food at home | plastic garbage in the sea

② reuse yarn | clean up the street regularly | use leftover food to feed animals | cut down on using plastic bottles

Let's Talk 1 💬

Work in pairs and talk about reducing garbage. Use expressions in Let's Practice 2 👥
for ① and ②.
Change roles.

〈 Example 〉

> A: 【 Did you knit your sweater? 】　　　　　　　　(Toolbox A)
>
> B: Yes, 【 I used yarn from my family's used sweaters. 】　(Toolbox B)
>
> 　　 We talked at school about how to reduce 【 ① 】.
>
> A: Yes.
>
> B: If we 【 ② 】, it will help reduce 【 ① 】.

Toolbox A 🔊

| 今日はノートなど授業用には何も持っていないね。 | You don't have any papers or notebooks for the class today. |
| 台所のごみは庭に持っていくのですか。 | Do you take food waste to the yard? |

Toolbox B

| タブレットしか持っていません。 | I only have my tablet. |
| 堆肥を作ります。 | I will make compost from it. |

Let's Listen 2 🎧 ANSWER THE QUESTIONS 🔊

Yumi is talking with Hayato.

1. He wants ☐ .

    ☐ (a) at least ten of them

    ☐ (b) at least twenty of them

    ☐ (c) as many as he can

2. ☐ (a) To collect garbage quickly and easily

    ☐ (b) To make the recycling rate go up

    ☐ (c) To put more garbage in each box

HAZARDOUS   PAPER   PLASTIC   ORGANIC   GLASS   E-WASTE   METAL

Let's Read ❷ 📖 ◀))

Read the passage with the graph and answers the questions.

People say the recycling rate in the fabric industry is still low. However, one company in Europe is famous because it is increasing its recycling rate steadily. The name of this company is Sunny Fabric Company. When it started recycling, it was very difficult to make good and beautiful fabrics. So, the staff worked very hard and they began to make new fabrics.

The fabrics didn't seem very beautiful at first, but some companies became interested in them because they were recycled. This was 15 years ago when the recycling rate was only 20%. Nine years ago, the company succeeded in making fabrics in beautiful red and blue. After that, they began to make fabrics of many colors and their recyling rate has been going up ever since.

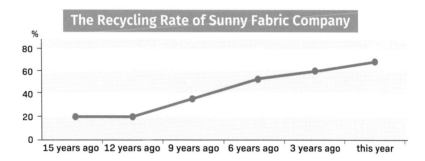

Words & Phrases ◀))

rate 割合   fabric industry 繊維産業   succeed-succeeded 成功する

1. Why is Sunny Fabric Company famous?

_____.

2. When it started to recycle, what was difficult?

_____.

3. Why were some companies interested in their fabrics?

_____.

4. What happened to the company nine years ago?

_____.

Let's Write ✏️

Do you have any good ideas for recycling? Write about how to recycle papers or plastics.

_____

_____

_____

Let's Talk 2 👥💬

Work in groups of three or more. Exchange ideas about recycling papers or plastics.
Tell the class about your group's discussion.

⟨Example⟩

In our group, _____

_____ .

📷 What do you see? Look at this photo and talk about it.

Part 2 Many sea animals are killed by the plastics in the ocean.

Let's Listen 🎧 ANSWER THE QUESTIONS 🔊

Yumi and Nanami are talking.

1. ☐ (a) A sea animal doctor

☐ (b) A marine scientist

☐ (c) An aquarium worker

2. ☐ (a) Many of them eat plastic garbage.

☐ (b) Sharks eat too much plastic garbage.

☐ (c) They can't find enough food.

Let's Read 1 🔊

（In an aquarium）

Yumi: Nanami, what are you looking at?

Nanami: Sea turtles. I like their motion. And their faces are so cute.

Yumi: You also like penguins?

Nanami: Yes, I like many sea animals. I want to be a marine scientist one day and help them.

Yumi: Why do you want to help them? Are they eaten by sharks?

Nanami: Ah, some of them are eaten by sharks. But that isn't a big problem. That's natural. There is another much more serious problem, plastic garbage in the ocean. Many sea animals are killed by the plastics in the ocean.

Yumi: What do you mean?

Nanami: Some die because they eat the garbage and their stomachs become full of them.

Yumi: Oh, then, they can't eat their own food. That's so sad.

Nanami: That's why I want to be a marine scientist. I want to find ways to reduce the plastic garbage in the ocean.

Words & Phrases 🔊

sea turtle ウミガメ   motion 動き   marine scientist 海洋科学者   *be* eaten 食われる   shark サメ

KEY PHRASES 🔊

What do you mean?

That's too sad.

That's why I want to be a marine scientist.

Let's Practice

Work in pairs and practice the conversation between Yumi and Nanami. Change roles.

Let's Talk 1

Work in pairs and share your opinion about garbage problems.
Change roles.

〈 Example 〉

A: I want to _____. (**Toolbox A**)

B: What [is the problem/are the problems]?

A: _____. (**Toolbox B**)

B: What do you mean?

A: _____. (Your [idea/reason])

B: It's _____. (**Toolbox C**)

A: That's why I want to _____.

Toolbox A

(I want to)	手伝う help	プラスチックの包装	plastic wrappings.
	減らす reduce	プラスチックごみのリサイクルの仕組み	the recycling system of plastic garbage.
	研究する study	環境への負荷が少ない衣服の素材	eco-friendly fabrics.
	調査する examine	マイクロプラスチックの人間への影響	microplastic's influence on humans.
	考案する invent	野生動物	wild animals.

Toolbox B

人々はゴミを持ち帰らない。　People don't take garbage back home.
人体に害があるそうだ。　I hear they are harmful to the human body.
リサイクル率が低いそうだ。　I hear the recycling rate is low.
日本では丁寧に包装されたものが多すぎる。　Many things are too carefully wrapped in Japan.
捨てられた服が環境問題になっている。　Clothes that are thrown away are an environmental problem.

Toolbox C

緊急の　　　　urgent
命に関わる　　fatal
健康に有害だ　harmful to our health
地球全体の問題　a global issue

Let's Read 2 📖

🔊

Read the passage and answer the questions.

Every living thing needs energy to live. Look around you. A plant needs energy, and so does an animal. Every one of them uses energy in everyday life. Plants get energy from the sun, water, and soil. Then some animals get energy from plants, and some eat other animals to get energy. This flow of energy is called the food chain.

Let's look at one example. Plankton in water is eaten by shrimp. The shrimp is eaten by small fish. The small fish is eaten by bigger fish like a mackerel, a tuna, or a salmon.

Do you know salmon go back to their birthplace to spawn? After spawning, they die and sink to the bottom of the river or float on water. Then, plankton, birds, or animals in the forest eat the dead bodies of the salmon. This may sound sad, but it is also a part of the food chain. If there's a problem in any part of the food chain, it affects all of the living things in the food chain and naturally they all suffer from it.

Words & Phrases
🔊

living thing 生き物　　energy エネルギー　　soil 土壌　　plankton プランクトン　　shrimp エビ

mackerel サバ　　tuna マグロ　　spawn 産卵する　　affect... …に影響する

1. What do plants get energy from?

_____.

2. What do animals get energy from?

_____.

3. What is the flow of energy called?

_____.

Let's Write ✏️

People say plastic garbage hurts the food chain. Think of a possible problem in the food chain and explain it.

_____

_____

_____

Let's Talk 2 🗣️

Work in groups of three or more. Exchange ideas about the food chain. Tell the class about your group's discussion.

〈Example〉

In our group, _____

_____ .

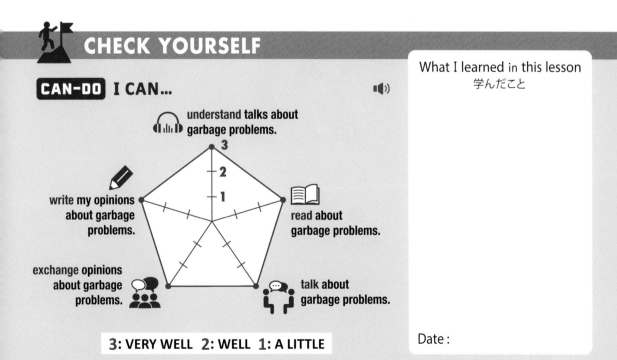

CHECK YOURSELF

CAN-DO I CAN... 🔊

understand **talks about garbage problems.**

write my opinions about garbage problems.

read **about garbage problems.**

exchange **opinions** about garbage problems.

talk **about garbage problems.**

3: VERY WELL 2: WELL 1: A LITTLE

What I learned in this lesson
学んだこと

Date :

Lesson 8
HEALTHCARE

CAN-DO

In this lesson, you will...

 listen **to talks** about healthcare.

 read **about** healthcare.

 talk **about** healthcare.

 exchange **opinions** about healthcare.

 write **your opinions** about healthcare.

Part 1 I hear a lot of people go to fitness clubs these days.

Let's Listen 1 🎧 ANSWER THE QUESTIONS 🔊

Nanami and Mr. King are talking.

1. Because [   ]

   ☐ (a) he can't drive

   ☐ (b) he wants to stay in shape

   ☐ (c) his hobby is cycling

2. She wonders [   ].

   ☐ (a) if people who go to fitness clubs are really concerned about their health

   ☐ (b) what kind of people go to fitness clubs

   ☐ (c) why fitness clubs are getting popular now

Let's Read 1 📖 🔊

Nanami: Mr. King, you usually come to school by bicycle. Is that for exercise?

Mr. King: Yes. I really need exercise to stay in shape. I can't move my body enough at school.

Nanami: I hear a lot of people go to fitness clubs these days. I wonder if they are really concerned about their health.

Mr. King: I think they are.

Nanami: Then, I wonder why some of them go on driving cars to work and also go to fitness clubs. I think they should change to bikes or public transportation. That would be better for their health, wouldn't it?

Mr. King: Definitely!

Words & Phrases 🔊

stay in shape よい体調でいる   fitness club フィットネスクラブ   I wonder if... …なのだろうか

be concerned about... …を気にしている   go on... …を続ける   I wonder why... どうして…なのだろうか

change to... …に換える   Definitely! その通りだ。

KEY PHRASES 🔊

I wonder if they are really concerned about their health.

I wonder why some of them go on driving cars to work.

Let's Practice 1 👥

Work in pairs and practice the conversation between Nanami and Mr. King.
Change roles.

Let's Practice 2 👫

Work in pairs. Practice the conversation as in the example.
Change roles.

〈 Example 〉

Ⓐ I hear it's good for our health	to sleep well.
	to exercise.
	to eat balanced meals.
	to reduce stress.
	to fast sometimes.

Ⓑ 1. I wonder if it really works. ➡ Ⓐ I (don't) think it really works.
　 2. I wonder why it works. ➡ 　 Let's ask ＿＿＿＿＿＿＿＿＿.
　 3. I wonder who said that. ➡ 　 ＿＿＿＿＿＿＿ told us about it.

Ⓑ We must try it out ourselves.

〈 fast 断食する 〉

Let's Talk 1 💬

Work in pairs and talk about what you are doing to stay in shape or to build up your strength.
Change roles.

〈 Example 〉

> A : Do you do anything to stay in shape or build up your strength?
>
> B : Well, I ＿＿＿＿＿＿＿＿＿＿＿＿＿＿＿＿＿＿＿＿.
>
> A : Does it work?
>
> B : [Yes. / Probably. / Well, I'm not sure. / I haven't noticed any changes yet.]

Toolbox 🔊

朝食に果物ジュースを飲んでいる	have fruit juice for breakfast
甘いものを食べない	not eat sweets
1日に約20回腕立て伏せをしている	do about 20 push-ups a day
11時以降は勉強しない	not study after 11 p.m.
ソフトドリンクを飲まない	cut out soft drinks
肉と野菜をたくさん食べている	eat a lot of meat and vegetables
放課後泳いでいる	swim after school
毎朝、駅まで走っている	run to the station every morning

Let's Listen **2** 🎧 ANSWER THE QUESTIONS 🔊

Rikuya and Nanami are talking.

1. They ☐⎯⎯☐.

    ☐ (a) go to a fitness club

    ☐ (b) go to a yoga class

    ☐ (c) run before breakfast

2. Because their new choice is free and they ☐⎯⎯☐

    ☐ (a) can do it in any weather

    ☐ (b) can do it together

    ☐ (c) can save money for a trip

Let's Read 2 📖 🔊

Read the passage with the graph and answer the questions.

Everyone wants to be healthy. Both men and women say walking or jogging is a good way to maintain their fitness level. They also admit getting enough sleep is probably the most natural and acceptable way of staying in shape. However, a recent report shows that they differ slightly in other ways of achieving this goal. Men rank training at a gym first, but women don't show much interest in it. Many men seem to try to stay in shape by setting aside a special day and time for training. On the other hand, many women rank sleeping first and eating healthy food very highly. Of course, there are some women who, in addition to these natural lifestyle choices, also join fitness classes such as yoga, indoor cycling, and swimming.

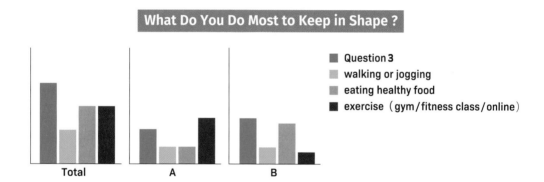

What Do You Do Most to Keep in Shape ?

■ Question 3
■ walking or jogging
■ eating healthy food
■ exercise（gym / fitness class / online）

Total　　A　　B

Words & Phrases 🔊

way　方法　　　rank ~ ...　～を…位にする　　　set ~ aside for...　～を…のために取っておく

1. What are the two most important things women do for their health?

_____ .

2. Which table shows the results for men, A or B?

_____ .

3 What activity does the blue bar show?

_____ .

Let's Write ✏️

Write about what you are doing to stay in shape or to build up strength.

Let's Talk 2 🗣️

Work in groups of three or more. Share your experience about staying in shape or building up strength. Tell the class about your group's discussion.

📷 What do you see? Look at this photo and talk about it.

Part **2** What will you do if you get sick?

Let's Listen 🎧 ANSWER THE QUESTIONS 🔊

Nanami and Mr. King are talking.

1. He ☐ .

    ☐ (a) asks the school nurse for help

    ☐ (b) goes to bed and takes his temperature

    ☐ (c) takes medicine and stays in bed

2. Because he ☐

    ☐ (a) doesn't like taking medicine

    ☐ (b) doesn't think his Japanese is good enough at a Japanese hospital

    ☐ (c) thinks it costs a lot to go to a hospital in Japan

Let's Read 1

Nanami: What do you usually do if you get sick?

Mr. King: First, I'll take medicine and stay in bed. But if it doesn't work, I'll ask someone like our school nurse for help.

Nanami: Don't you go to a hospital?

Mr. King: Well, I try not to go to a hospital. I'm not sure if I can explain my condition clearly in Japanese. It may be difficult for me to understand everything the doctor asks or tells me.

Nanami: Hmm. There's a hospital near the city hall where the doctor speaks English. There's also a pharmacy next to it.

Mr. King: Thanks. I'll go there next time.

Words & Phrases

get sick 病気になる   take medicine 薬を服用する   try not to... …しないように努力する   pharmacy 薬局

KEY PHRASES

I'm not sure if I can explain my condition clearly in Japanese.

It may be difficult for me to understand everything the doctor asks or tells me.

Let's Practice

Work in pairs and practice the conversation between Nanami and Mr. King.
Change roles.

Let's Talk **1**

Work in pairs and share what you are doing to stay in shape and what you usually do when you get sick.

Change roles.

〈Example〉

> A: Are you doing something to stay in shape?
>
> B: I _____. _____. (*Comment*)
>
> A: I see. What if you get sick? What do you usually do?
>
> B: I _____. _____. (*Comment*)

Let's Read 2 📖

Read the passage with the graph and answer the questions.

　　The number of foreign workers and residents in our country has been increasing rapidly. In response to this, the number of hospitals with doctors and nurses who have multi-language skills has also increased. However, it still hasn't caught up with the growing need. Other medical workers must also be ready to meet these new language challenges.

　　Normally, there are few pharmacies where the staff can help in English, much less in other languages. Non-Japanese speakers tend to hesitate to go to pharmacies without a prescription from a doctor.

　　Tablet computers will become strong communication tools in such cases. Information booklets and online Japanese lessons, especially for emergency purposes, will also help. In these ways, we can make a more secure society for all the residents of Japan.

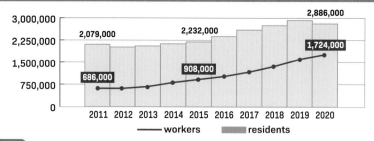

Annual Change of Foreign Workers & Residents in the Past 10 Years

workers　　residents

Words & Phrases

foreign　外国籍の　　resident　居住者　　in response to...　…に応えて　　much less...　ましてや…ではない

hesitate　ためらう　　prescription　処方箋

1. How has the population of foreign workers changed in our country?

_____.

2. Why do non-Japanese speakers tend to hesitate to go to pharmacies?

_____.

3. List and briefly explain three ways we can make a more secure society for foreign workers and residents of Japan.

_____

_____

_____.

Let's Write ✏️

Write your opinion on what you think we should do to stay in shape.

_____

_____

_____

_____

Let's Talk 2 💬

Work in groups of three or more and talk about what you wrote above. Tell the class about your group's discussion.

〈Example〉

_____ thinks we should _____ to stay in shape.

_____ . (*Comment*)

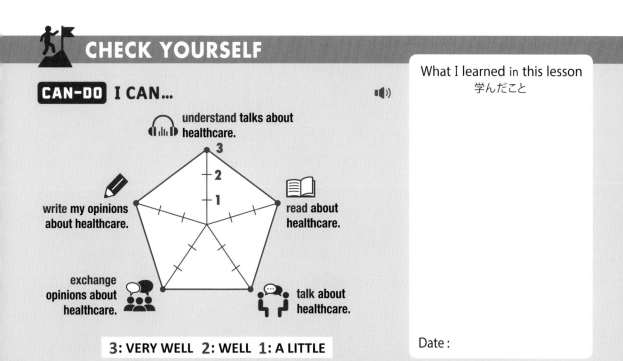

🚩 CHECK YOURSELF

CAN-DO I CAN... 🔊

- understand talks about healthcare.
- read about healthcare.
- talk about healthcare.
- exchange opinions about healthcare.
- write my opinions about healthcare.

3
2
1

3: VERY WELL 2: WELL 1: A LITTLE

What I learned in this lesson
学んだこと

Date :

ONLINE ACTIVITIES

CAN-DO

In this lesson, you will...

 listen to talks about online activities.

 read about online activities.

 talk about online activities.

 exchange opinions about online activities.

 write your opinions about online activities.

Part 1   Do you often use online shopping?

Let's Listen 1 🎧 ANSWER THE QUESTIONS 🔊

Yumi and Eric are talking.

1. Because they [   ]

   ☐ (a) don't have time to go shopping

   ☐ (b) don't know how to shop online

   ☐ (c) can get items more cheaply

2. She thinks it is [   ] .

   ☐ (a) not easy to shop online

   ☐ (b) useful for some people

   ☐ (c) not popular

Let's Read 1 📖 🔊

Yumi: That T-shirt looks good on you, Eric. Where did you get it?

Eric: My father bought it online.

Yumi: Cool! Do you often use online shopping?

Eric: Yes, we do. We buy many things online. Online shops often sell items at lower prices. They have more choices, too. How about you, Yumi?

Yumi: My family doesn't do much online shopping. We like "going" shopping. We want to see and touch the actual items before we buy them.

Eric: I see your point, but I think online shopping will be even more popular in the future.

Yumi: Why do you think so?

Eric: Because it's so convenient. We can get anything easily and quickly.

Yumi: I agree with you. It's especially useful for older people or busy people.

Words & Phrases 🔊

items 品物　　at lower prices より低価格で　　more choices より多くの選択肢　　actual 実際の

KEY PHRASES 🔊

I see your point, but I think online shopping will be even more popular in the future.
I agree with you.

Let's Practice 1 👥

Work in pairs and practice the conversation between Yumi and Eric.
Change roles.

Let's Practice 2 👥

Work in pairs. Practice the conversation as in the example.
Change roles.

〈 Example 〉

> A: I [think / don't think] <u>online shopping</u> will be more popular.
>
> B: [I agree with you. / I see your point, but I don't think so. /
>
>   I see your point, but I think it will become even more popular.]

 online games

 online movies & TV programs

 e-sports

Let's Talk 1 💬

Work in pairs and talk about online shopping.
Change roles.

〈 Example 〉

> A: Do you think online shopping will become even more popular in the future?
>
> B: _____.
>
> A: Why do you think so?
>
> B: Because _____. How about you?
>
> A: [I agree / I disagree].
>
> B: Can you tell me why?
>
> A: It's because _____.

Toolbox 🔊

［早く／簡単に］物を手に入れることができる	can get things [quickly/easily]
…にとって便利だ	it is convenient for…
買い物に行く方が楽しい	it is more fun to go shopping
オンラインショップを使うのは難しい	it is difficult to use online shops
ときどき間違った商品が届く	we sometimes receive the wrong items
返品するのが面倒だ	it is troublesome to return items
安い偽物の商品がある	there are some cheap copies
全ての売り手を信用できるわけではない	we can't trust all the sellers

Let's Listen 2 🎧 ANSWER THE QUESTIONS 🔊

Yumi and Eric are talking.

1. ☐ (a) He doesn't like the color.

   ☐ (b) They are too small.

   ☐ (c) They are too big.

2. He should [　　　].

   ☐ (a) try on the shoes next time

   ☐ (b) contact the online store

   ☐ (c) not use online shopping

Let's Read 2

Read the passage with the graph and answer the questions.

These days, many people use online shopping. We can buy various items online such as books, clothes, shoes, furniture, and food. Online shopping is especially popular with older people because they don't have to carry heavy shopping bags. It is also popular among parents with small children because they can shop anytime and anywhere; they don't have to bring their children shopping. Many supermarkets have started online shopping and delivery service. By doing so, they try to attract new customers.

What Do People Buy Online?

- Others 5%
- Furniture 10%
- Food 15%
- Books & Magazines 40%
- Clothes & Shoes 30%

Words & Phrases

furniture 家具　　anytime いつでも　　delivery service 配達サービス　　attract 引き寄せる
customers 客

1. What do people buy most online?

_____.

2. Why is online shopping popular with older people?

_____.

3. Why is online shopping popular among parents with small children?

_____.

4. How do many supermarkets try to attract new customers?

_____.

Let's Write ✏️

Do you think online shopping will be even more popular in the future? Why do you think so?

_____

_____

_____

Let's Talk 2 💬

Work in groups of three or more. Talk about your ideas about online shopping. Tell the class about your group's discussion.

〈 Example 〉

In our group, _____ think online shopping will become even more popular.

It is because _____ .

> all of us / most of us / some of us / a few of us / none of us

📷 **What do you see?**   Look at this photo and talk about it.

Part 2 | We can learn new things and skills through the internet.

Let's Listen 🎧 ANSWER THE QUESTIONS 🔊

Sayaka and Jon are talking.

1. He ⬚ .

☐ (a) listens to the lectures

☐ (b) chooses the course and studies it

☐ (c) practices speaking with the teacher

2. He ⬚ .

☐ (a) doesn't have classmates

☐ (b) can ask the teacher questions

☐ (c) can study in his free time

Let's Read 1

Sayaka: Jon, what do you think about online learning?

Jon: It's good because we can learn new things and skills through the internet.

Sayaka: Can you give me an example?

Jon: Sure. For example, I'm taking online lessons to practice my Japanese. I go to the website, choose a course, and study it.

Sayaka: Do you like it?

Jon: Yes, I do. It's very useful. I don't have to go to a classroom, so I can take lessons in my room when I have free time.

Sayaka: I see. Online learning has some good points. Are there any bad points?

Jon: Let me see. Well, I don't have any classmates, so it is sometimes difficult to keep up my motivation. And it would be nice to practice conversation with a partner.

Sayaka: Well, you can practice with me anytime.

Words & Phrases

keep up *one's* motivation （ ＝ [*be* / stay] motivated） やる気を維持する

KEY PHRASES

Can you give me an example?

For example, I'm taking online lessons to practice my Japanese.

Let's Practice

Work in pairs and practice the conversation between Sayaka and Jon. Change roles.

Let's Talk 1

Work in pairs and talk about good points and bad points about online learning.
Change roles.

〈 Example 〉

> A: What do you think about online learning?
>
> B: I think online learning has some [good / bad] points.
>
> A: Can you give me an example?
>
> B: Sure. For example, _____.

Toolbox

［いつでも／どこでも］勉強できる	can study ［ anytime / anywhere ］
自分のペースで勉強できる	can study at *one's* own pace
先生に質問しにくい	not easy to ask the teacher questions
本当にやる気がないとダメです。	have to be really motivated
会話する相手がいない	don't have a conversation partner

Let's Read 2 📖 🔊

Read the webpage and answer the questions.

Our website has offered a wide variety of online courses since 2000. They are suitable for learning new skills, gaining more knowledge, advancing your career, and more. Many young people take our practical courses, for example, cooking and web design. They can get certificates after completing these courses. Our online program is popular with older people, too. They study languages, history, and arts. Many office workers take our business courses so that they can improve their careers. In particular, they are interested in developing their leadership skills. We also offer some courses for children. For example, we have English and science classes for them. If you are interested, try our trial lesson for free!

openseas.com **Online Courses**

Find your courses

☐ Computer ☐ Language ☐ Business ☐ Children
☐ History ☐ Arts ☐ Food & Health ☐ Others

Top 3 Online Courses

1. Travel English（Language） 5.0 ☆☆☆☆☆
2. Improving Leadership Skills（Business） 4.5 ☆☆☆☆☆
3. Introduction to Japanese Modern Art（Arts） 4.0 ☆☆☆☆☆

Words & Phrases 🔊

offer 提供する

a wide variety of... 幅広い種類の…

be suitable for... …に適している

gain 得る

advance *one's* career キャリアを積む

practical 実用的な

web design ウェブデザイン

certificates 証明書

complete 完了する

trial lesson 体験授業

1. What is the third most popular online course?

_____.

2. How can people get certificates?

_____.

3. Why do many office workers take business courses?

_____.

4. What kind of online course would you like to take? Why?

_____.

Let's Write ✎

Do you think more people will use online learning? Why or why not?

_____

_____

_____

Let's Talk 2

Work in groups of three or more. Exchange ideas about online learning. Tell the class about your group's discussion.

〈 Example 〉

In our group, _____

_____ .

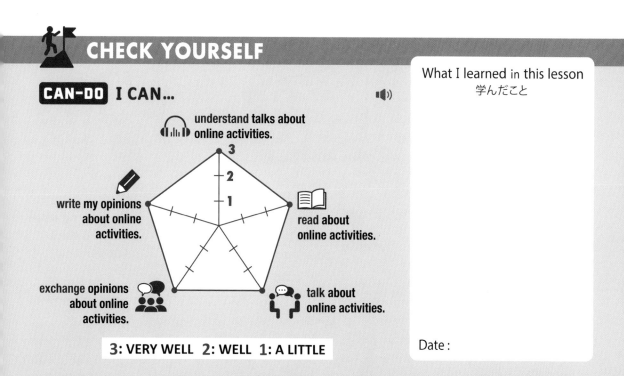

🏃🚩 **CHECK YOURSELF**

CAN-DO I CAN... 🔊

understand talks about online activities.

write my opinions about online activities.

read about online activities.

exchange opinions about online activities.

talk about online activities.

3
2
1

3: VERY WELL 2: WELL 1: A LITTLE

What I learned in this lesson
学んだこと

Date :

Lesson 10
INFORMATION SKILLS

CAN-DO

In this lesson, you will...

 listen to talks about the ways people use media.

 read about the ways people use media.

 talk about the ways you use media.

 exchange opinions about the ways people use media.

 write your opinions about the ways you use media.

Part 1 | I mainly get information from TV or online.

Let's Listen 1 ANSWER THE QUESTIONS

Ms. Kimura and Jon are talking.

1. Jon mainly gets it from [ ].

- ☐ (a) books or magazines
- ☐ (b) the radio or newspapers
- ☐ (c) TV or online

2. Because it's published [ ]

- ☐ (a) as printed material and no one can change it later
- ☐ (b) from several newspaper companies and we can compare them
- ☐ (c) only after the editors check it carefully

Let's Read 1 📖 🔊

Ms. Kimura: What kind of media do you use to get information?

Jon: It depends on the topic, but I mainly get information from TV or online.

Ms. Kimura: Don't you read newspapers?

Jon: Yes, I do, but not every day. I think they are useful to know about things not so urgent but important to our life.

Ms. Kimura: Right. I think their information is reliable. It's published only after the editors check it carefully.

Jon: I didn't know that. Anyway, when I want to know something as quickly as possible, I check it online. The results of baseball games, for example.

Words & Phrases 🔊

media （マス）メディア　　It depends on the topic. 話題によります。　　urgent 緊急の　　reliable 信頼できる
publish 発行する　　editor 編集者

KEY PHRASE 🔊

Don't you read newspapers?

Let's Practice 1 👥

Work in pairs and practice the conversation between Ms. Kimura and Jon.
Change roles.

Let's Practice 2 👥

Work in pairs. Ask questions and reply as in the example.
Change roles.

〈Example〉

A: What kind of media do you use to get information?

B: I │ read [books / magazines / newspapers].

　　 │ watch [television / movies].

　　 │ listen to the radio.

　　 │ use the internet.

A: I see. Don't you _____?

B: [Yes, I _____, too. / No, I don't _____.]

Let's Talk 1 💬

Work in pairs and talk about your favorite media.
Change roles.

〈Example〉

A: To get information,

　 I often │ read [books / magazines / newspapers].

　　　　　 │ watch [television / movies].

　　　　　 │ listen to the radio.

　　　　　 │ use the internet.

B: Why do you use [it / them]?

A: It's because _____.

Toolbox 🔊

その情報は[偏っていない ／ 最新 ／ 特定の話題に焦点が絞られている]。

　The information is [impartial / up-to-date / focused on a particular topic].

[自分のペースで ／ 好きな時にどこでも ／ 他のことをしながら] 情報を入手できる。

　I can get information [at my own pace / anytime and anywhere / while doing other things].

Let's Listen 2 🎧 ANSWER THE QUESTIONS 🔊

Nanami and Mr. King are talking.

1. Because she wanted to see the games ☐☐☐☐

    ☐ (a) among people who didn't know her

    ☐ (b) on a big screen

    ☐ (c) together with other people

2. To ☐☐☐ was important to her.

    ☐ (a) know the results

    ☐ (b) share the feeling of being together

    ☐ (c) watch them in real time

Let's Read 2 📖 🔊

Read the passage with the graph and answer the questions.

Here is a summary of surveys on how much time people spent on TV, radio, online, and newspapers on weekdays between 2016 and 2020.

First, we see that the time we spend on online media is increasing year by year. Many people think it will soon surpass the time spent watching TV. People want more specific and personalized information on demand now.

Second, people spend a lot less time on newspapers and the radio than on the other two media, but the amount of time has not changed much over the past five years.

Why, then, do people spend more time listening to the radio than reading newspapers? Maybe it's because newspaper headlines help us choose the articles we want to spend time reading. On the other hand, when we want to get some information through a radio program, we have to listen from beginning to end, which takes longer than scanning a newspaper.

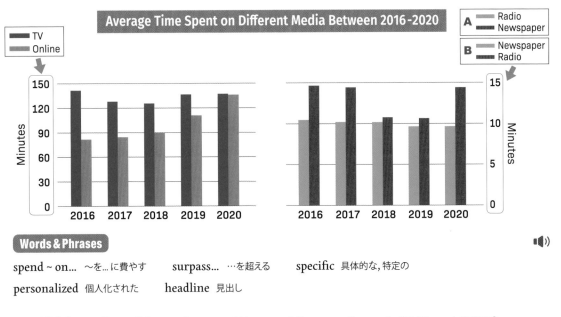

Words & Phrases 🔊

spend ~ on... 〜を…に費やす　　surpass... …を超える　　specific 具体的な, 特定の

personalized 個人化された　　headline 見出し

1. Which medium did people spend the most time on through 2016 and 2020?

_____.

2. Which color bars show the time spent on radio and newspaper, **A** or **B**?

_____.

3. What does the writer think is the reason behind the increase in the use of online media?

_____.

Let's Write ✏️

Write about the media you often use.

_____

_____

_____

Let's Talk 2 👥💬

Work in groups of three or more. Share your ideas about the media you often use. Tell the class about your group's discussion.

📷 **What do you see?** Look at this photo and talk about it.

Part 2 | Why are good information skills important?

Let's Listen 🎧 ANSWER THE QUESTIONS 🔊

Mr. King and Nanami are talking.

1. She usually [ ].

☐ (a) checks an encyclopedia

☐ (b) looks for someone who seems to know it

☐ (c) searches the internet

2. He usually [ ].

☐ (a) checks its URL and who created the site

☐ (b) looks for someone who seems to know about it

☐ (c) visits other sites and sometimes checks other media

Let's Read 1 📖 🔊

Mr. King:	When you want to find information about something, what do you do first?
Nanami:	To start, I usually search the internet using key words that seem to lead me to sites I want to go to.
Mr. King:	Are you always satisfied with the sites you arrive at?
Nanami:	In most cases, yes. However, sometimes I wonder whether I can believe all the contents or not.
Mr. King:	So do I. In such cases, I always visit other sites. I sometimes check other media, too.
Nanami:	The internet is really a useful tool, but we should check and supplement the contents we find there by using other media.

Words & Phrases 🔊

be satisfied with... …に満足する   in most cases ほとんどの場合   contents 内容, 中身
So do I. 私もそうだ。   supplement... …を補う

KEY PHRASE 🔊

In such cases, I always visit other sites.

Let's Practice 👥

Work in pairs and practice the conversation between Mr. King and Nanami. Change roles.

Let's Talk 1

Work in pairs and share your opinions on checking the information you find. Change roles.

〈 Example 〉

A: What do you do
when you think
the information you get from

a book		biased *
a magazine		not objective
a newspaper	is	not up to date
television		unreliable
the radio		partial
the internet		useless

?

B: I usually check to see if there are other sites on the same or similar subject.

* 偏っている ／ 客観的でない ／ 古い ／ 信頼できない ／ 部分的な ／ 役に立たない

Toolbox

いつアップデートされたか調べる	check when it was updated
書いた人の名前が載っているか調べる	check if it gives the writer's name
関連したサイトの情報が記載されているか調べる	check if it gives information on related sites
情報の出典が載っているか調べる	check if it gives the source of information
無視して他を探す	ignore it and look for another source

Let's Read 2 📖 🔊

Read the passage and answer the questions.

There are a lot of different sources of information available to everyone in our society today. What or who do you rely on most when you want to get information?

According to a recent age-group survey, there are some noteworthy differences in different age groups' behavior toward face-to-face interaction and the use of online and printed media. Age groups were divided into the following six sets: children, students, 18-29, 30-49, 50-65, and over 65. Let's take a brief look at some of the findings. 5

Children not yet in junior high school get most of their information or learn things directly from other family members, especially parents, or from their teachers. As they grow up these influences become less important, and the percentages of printed and online media use go up. 10

The use of the internet reaches its peak in the age group between 18 and 29. In the age group between 30 and 49, printed materials — for example, books and magazines — become more important. However, this age group still uses online media more than these printed materials. People in the age group between 50 and 65 show a rather balanced behavior toward online and offline media. However, the oldest group over 65 doesn't show much 15 interest in using online media, probably because they have never received proper computer literacy training.

The role of teachers is quite significant as an information source in most age groups. When students receive face-to-face instruction from teachers in a classroom, they are not only recipients of the information, but they also learn how to use this information 20 correctly. Some of the students may, in due course, want to become teachers themselves.

Whatever sources of information you may use, it is essential to keep the following in mind to develop good information skills for today's information society.

- Use a variety of information sources and try to have well-balanced viewpoints.
- Be able to judge whether the information is reliable. 25
- Be able to add to your key knowledge and always update it.
- Gain confidence in your ability to use the information you get wisely.

Words & Phrases 🔊

noteworthy 注目に値する　　face-to-face interaction 対面でのやりとり　　reach *one's* peak ピークに達する

computer literacy コンピュータ運用能力　　significant 重要な　　recipient 受取人

in due course やがて, 時が来れば　　whatever... どんな…を　　wisely 上手に

1. What is the biggest difference between the age groups 50-65 and over 65 in choosing information media?

_____ .

2. What is the most important thing you consider when you choose an information source? Why?

_____ .

Let's Write ✏

What media do you use to get information? Write your opinion with a good example.

_____

_____

_____

Let's Talk 2 💬

Work in groups of three or more. Discuss your ideas about ways to get information. Tell the class about your group's discussion.

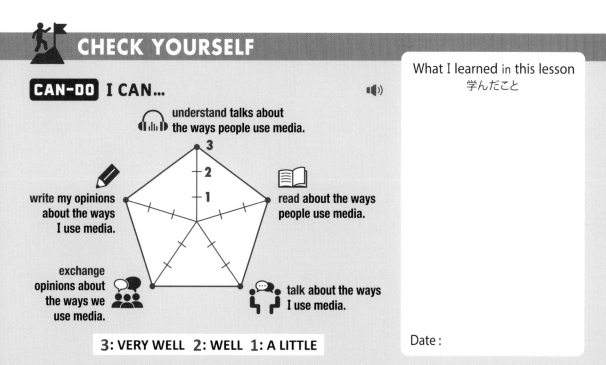

🏃 **CHECK YOURSELF**

CAN-DO I CAN... 🔊

understand talks about the ways people use media.

write my opinions about the ways I use media.

read about the ways people use media.

exchange opinions about the ways we use media.

talk about the ways I use media.

3: VERY WELL 2: WELL 1: A LITTLE

What I learned in this lesson
学んだこと

Date :

【著者】
　高田三夫
　石川和弘
　柳瀬和明
　柳田恵美子
　萱忠義
　齋藤雪絵
　Colette Morin

【編集・執筆協力】
　佐伯林規江

【表紙デザイン・イラスト】
　デザインスタジオ・maru　丸田薫

【本文デザイン】
　京都文英堂　株式会社　反保文江

【ウェブディレクター】
　株式会社 office masui　益井貴生

【音声編集】
　シンプティースタジオ　粕谷和弘

写真・図版提供
　アドビ　株式会社
　株式会社　アマナイメージズ
　国際連合食糧農業機関（FAO）

Open Seas for Global Friendships III

2023 年 10 月 1 日　　第 1 刷発行

監修者　上智大学名誉教授　吉田　研作
　　　　上智大学教授　　　藤田　保

発行所　京都文英堂株式会社
　　　　〒601-8372　京都市南区吉祥院嶋高町12番地
　　　　（代表）075-661-9960

販　売　株式会社　文英堂

印刷所　株式会社　天理時報社

Class   No.   Name

Lesson **1** MAKING A PRESENTATION

Lesson **2** TRADITIONAL CULTURES

Lesson **3** PET BUSINESSES

Lesson **4** FAVORITE BOOKS & MAGAZINES

Lesson **5** TAKING A TRIP